John M Armleder

CA. CA.

Herausgeben von / Edited by
Ingrid Pfeiffer

Schirn Kunsthalle Frankfurt
edition cantz

Die Publikation wird gefördert durch Mitglieder des Kuratoriums und des Vorstands des Vereins der Freunde der Schirn Kunsthalle e.V. /
The publication is supported by the members of the Board of Trustees and of the Executive Board of the Verein der Freunde der Schirn Kunsthalle e.V.

Die Ausstellung wird unterstützt von /
The exhibition is supported by

SCHIRN ZEITGENOSSEN prohelvetia

Inhalt / Contents

5 Geleitwort
Christian Strenger

7 Vorwort
Philipp Demandt

12 Zitat – Zufall – Ironie
John M Armleders Kunst der offenen Kommunikation
Ingrid Pfeiffer

20 Biografie
Rebecca Herlemann

60 Bibliografie

62 Werkliste

63 Impressum

43 Preface
Christian Strenger

45 Foreword
Philipp Demandt

50 Quote—Chance—Irony
John M Armleder's Art of Open Communication
Ingrid Pfeiffer

58 Biography
Rebecca Herlemann

60 Bibliography

62 List of Works

63 Colophon

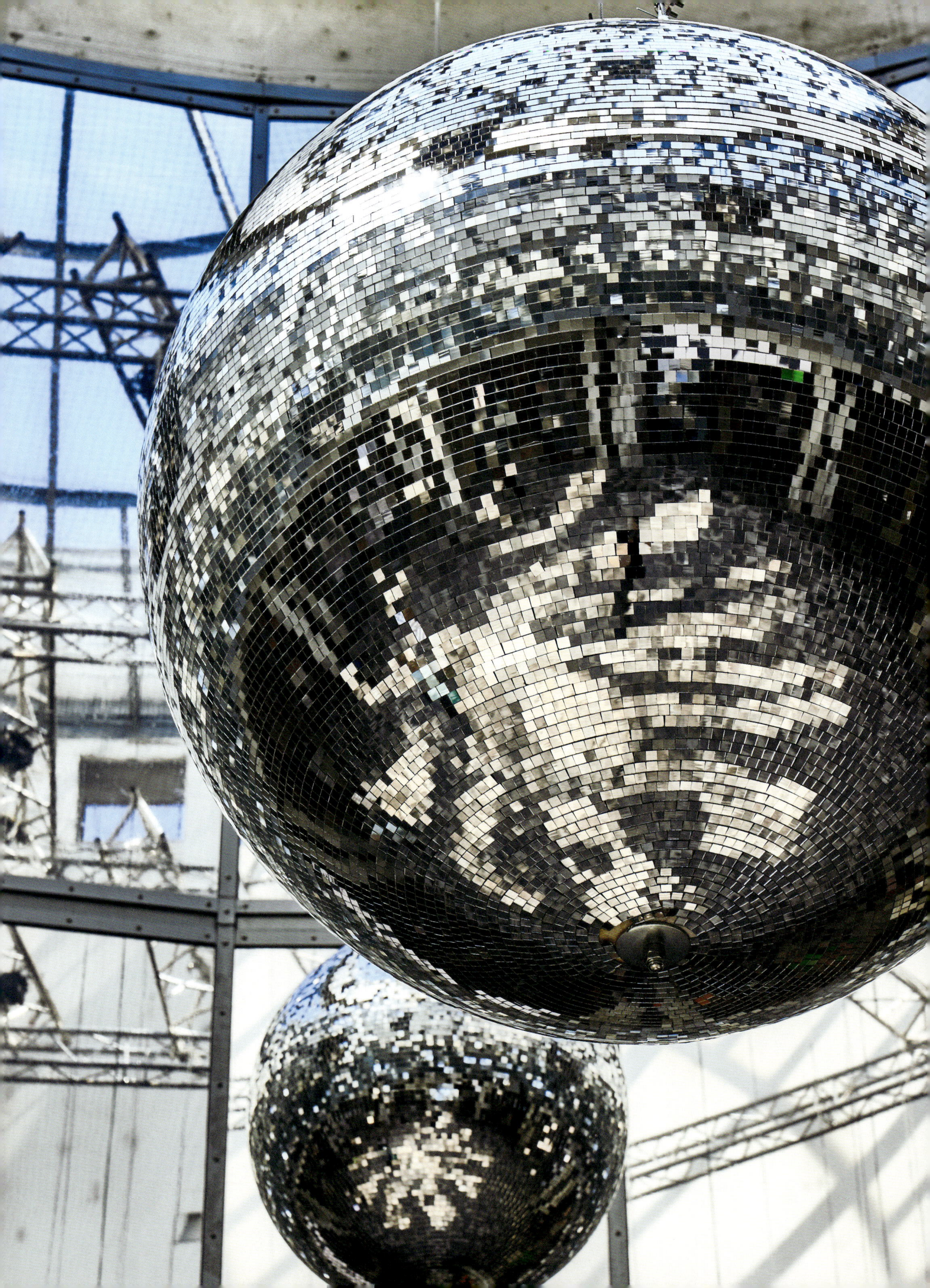

Geleitwort

Es gibt wohl nichts, was John M Armleder nicht kann. Seine Kunst verbindet Hochkultur und Alltägliches, integriert Tiefgründiges sowie Banales und eröffnet einen vielfältigen Kosmos kunsthistorischer Bezüge. Design, Op- und Pop-Art, Konstruktivismus und die enge Verwandtschaft zur Fluxus-Bewegung – all das zeigt sich in Armleders weitreichendem Œuvre, ganz zu schweigen von seinen ironischen wie poetischen Aperçus zur heutigen Kunstwelt, die er lässig einzustreuen vermag.

Als einer der wichtigsten Konzept-, Performance- und Objektkünstler seiner Zeit ist er schon jetzt Teil der Kunstgeschichte. Mit den für die Schirn entwickelten Installationen schafft er uns ein besonderes Ausstellungserlebnis: Zwanzig Discokugeln machen die Schirn Rotunde zu einem Spiegelsaal, farbig leuchtende *Pour Paintings* treten neben raumfüllende Wandarbeiten und Skulpturen.

Armleders Spiel mit dem Zufall, seine Strategie der Verschleierung und Spontaneität sorgen für Überraschung und (Er-)Staunen. Damit bindet er die Betrachter aktiv ein. Die Arbeit wird so zum »Event«, wie er selbst einmal sagte. Die fast 2.300 Schirn Freunde freuen sich, diese Reise durch die Kunstgeschichte des 20. und 21. Jahrhunderts intensiv zu unterstützen. Obwohl Armleders Werk alles Herkömmliche ablehnt, erscheint die Kunst des 70-Jährigen in ihren zeitgenössischen und kunsthistorischen Bezügen perfekt inszeniert und wird uns Freunde der Schirn begeistern!

Christian Strenger
Schirn Freunde e.V.

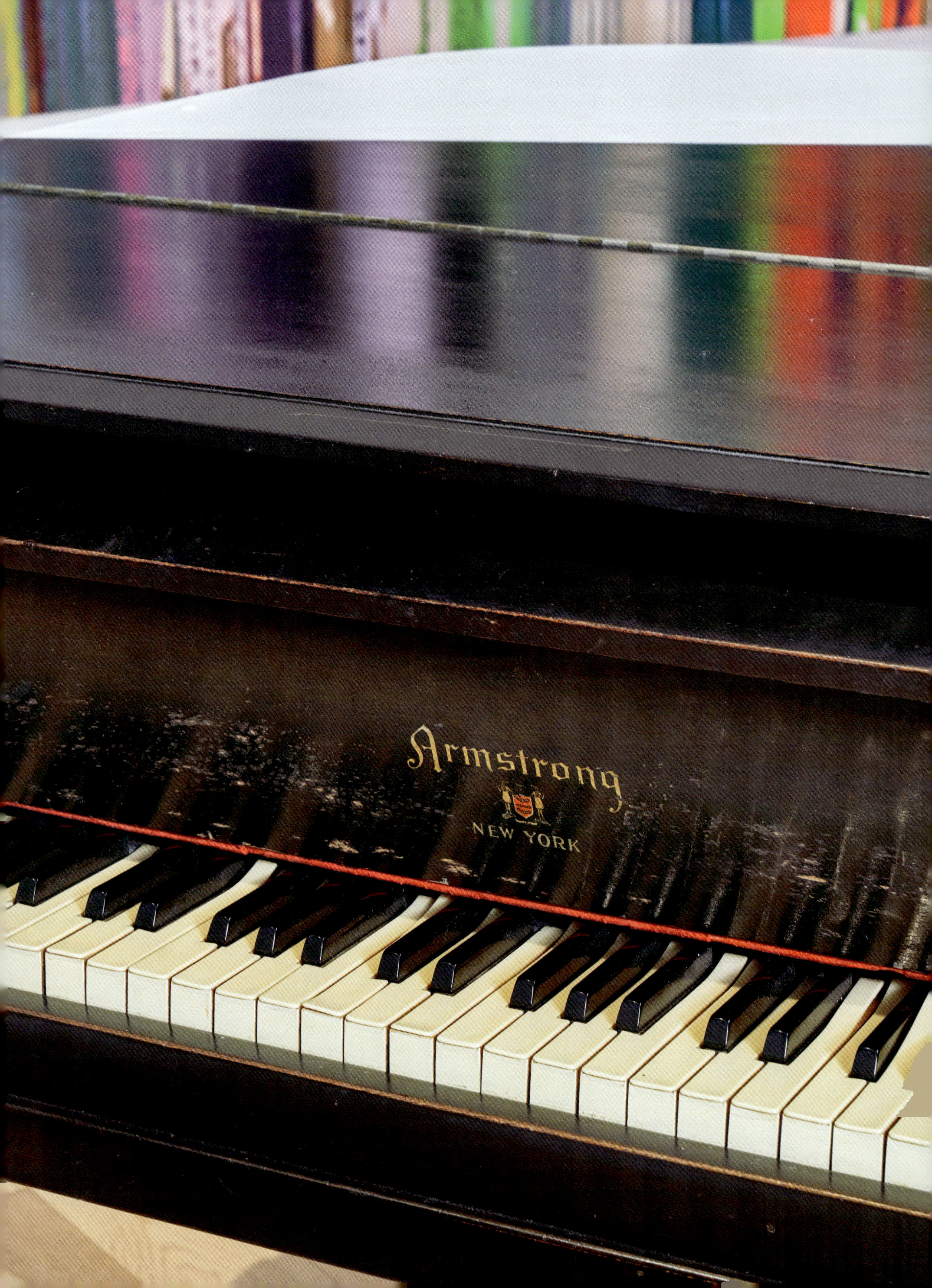
Armstrong
NEW YORK

Vorwort

Es gehört zum Programm der Schirn Kunsthalle Frankfurt, immer wieder Künstlerinnen und Künstler zu präsentieren, die in Deutschland länger nicht gezeigt wurden und deren beruflicher Höhepunkt oder deren prominenteste Phase bereits einige Jahre zurückliegen. Die Wieder- und Neubetrachtung unter veränderten Bedingungen und in einem veränderten zeitgenössischen Kontext hat in der Vergangenheit oft zu einer interessanten Befragung ihrer aktuellen Bedeutung geführt, so etwa bei Julian Schnabel, A.R. Penck und Peter Halley.

John M Armleder ist einer der einflussreichsten zeitgenössischen Künstler in Europa. Seine ungewöhnlichen Arbeiten fußen auf dem formalen Repertoire der Moderne – Konstruktivismus, Op-Art, Pop, gestische abstrakte Malerei, aber auch Video und Design. Der Künstler vermengt kunsthistorische Referenzen aus allen Epochen mit Humor und findet poetische oder ironische Kommentare zu unserer heutigen Wirklichkeit und dem Status der Kunst. Mit einer großen medialen Bandbreite vermischt Armleder Hochkultur und Alltägliches, Zufall und Planung, Tiefgründiges und Banales und verbindet es zu einem ambivalenten und einzigartigen Erlebnis.

Bereits zweimal war das Werk von John M Armleder in Gruppenausstellungen in der Schirn zu sehen, allerdings liegt das schon sehr lange zurück: 1986 in der Reihe *Prospect* und 1998 in *Freie Sicht aufs Mittelmeer,* einer Kooperation mit dem Kunsthaus Zürich. Die letzte Einzelausstellung von Armleder in Deutschland war 2006 im Kunstverein in Hannover. Zu seinem 70. Geburtstag 2018 hatte er zwei größere Ausstellungen im Museum Madre in Neapel und im Museion in Bozen.

Für die Rotunde und den großen Saal in der Schirn hat John M Armleder zwei neue Installationen konzipiert, die er unter dem Titel *CA.CA.* zusammenfasst. Es gehört zum Grundprinzip des 1948 in Genf geborenen Künstlers, sich aktiv auf jeden neuen Ort einzulassen und mit den jeweils vorliegenden Bedingungen zu arbeiten. Dafür verwendet Armleder oft Versatzstücke aus früheren Installationen und mischt unterschiedlichste Materialien und Medien miteinander.

Ich möchte John M Armleder meinen ausdrücklichen Dank für sein großes Engagement bei der Ausstellungsvorbereitung und bei der Realisierung seines eindrucksvollen Werks in der Schirn aussprechen. Seinen außerordentlichen Einsatz und wertvollen Beitrag zur Umsetzung dieser herausragenden Ausstellung wissen wir sehr zu schätzen. Ebenso danken wir seinen Assistenten Lena Guévry und Ludovic Bourilly für ihre zuverlässige Mitarbeit.

Ganz besonders danke ich der Kuratorin Ingrid Pfeiffer, die dieses ambitionierte Projekt in engem Austausch mit dem Künstler konzipiert hat. Ihre große Einsatzbereitschaft bei der umfassenden Ausstellungsvorbereitung und aufwendigen Umsetzung wird durch ihre intensive Recherche zum Werk und Schaffen Armleders untermauert, die sich auch in ihrem differenzierten, bereichernden Text im vorliegenden Katalog spiegelt. Als kuratorische Assistenz stand Rebecca Herlemann ihr mit großem Engagement zur Seite, ihr gilt ebenso mein herzlicher Dank für ihren Einsatz sowie für ihren Textbeitrag zur Ausstellungspublikation.

Das aufmerksame Lektorat der vorliegenden Texte ist Karin Osbahr und Lizzie Gilbert zu verdanken, Gérard Goodrow danke ich für die sensible Übersetzung der Texte. Ausdrücklich danken möchte ich der Edition Cantz für die gute Zusammenarbeit, insbesondere Doris Hansmann. Nicht minder gilt mein Dank Maik Stapelberg und Daniel Fritz von stapelberg&fritz für die kreative Gestaltung der Publikation. Die stimmige und besondere Ausstellungsgestaltung ist darüber hinaus John Russo von Studioheyhey zu verdanken. Norbert Miguletz danke ich ausdrücklich für die gelungenen Aufnahmen von John M Armleders Werken in der Schirn.

Ebenso gilt mein ausdrücklicher Dank Mehdi Chouakri. Für seine wertvolle Unterstützung bei der Ausstellungskonzeption sowie seinen Rat und Einsatz bei der Kommunikation mit dem Künstler und seinem Atelier bin ich äußerst dankbar. Ich bedanke mich außerdem bei der David Kordansky Gallery LA für die gute Zusammenarbeit und freundliche Unterstützung.

Den Schirn Zeitgenossen möchte ich außerdem herzlich danken, einem Kreis privater Förderer, die wiederholt eine zeitgenössische Ausstellung in der Schirn großzügig unterstützen, sowie der Schweizer Kulturstiftung Pro Helvetia, die für das Zustandekommen der Ausstellung ebenfalls einen erheblichen Beitrag leistet. Weiterhin haben Mitglieder des Kuratoriums und des Vorstands vom Verein der Freunde der Schirn Kunsthalle e.V. mit ihren zahlreichen Spenden die Realisation der begleitenden Publikation maßgeblich gefördert. Stellvertretend möchte ich insbesondere dem Vorsitzenden Christian Strenger und der Geschäftsführerin Tamara Fürstin von Clary ein großes Dankeschön für ihr persönliches Engagement aussprechen.

Danken möchte ich des Weiteren der Stadt Frankfurt, stellvertretend für alle Entscheidungsträger dem Oberbürgermeister Peter Feldmann und der Kulturdezernentin Ina Hartwig für ihre fortwährende Unterstützung unserer Arbeit in der Schirn.

Dieses herausragende Ausstellungsprojekt und die vorliegende Publikation wäre ohne das engagierte Team der Schirn nicht zustande gekommen. Dafür möchte ich allen Mitarbeiterinnen und Mitarbeitern meinen großen Dank aussprechen: zunächst der Ausstellungsleiterin Esther Schlicht mit Anna Noll sowie Karin Grüning, Elke Walter und Luise Leyer für ihre Koordination des Transports sowie für den Ausstellungsauf- und abbau. Christian Teltz und Oliver Taschke danke ich für die technische Betreuung, ebenso wie Andreas Gundermann und dem Hängeteam sowie der Restauratorin Susanne Silbernagel. Das ausgefallene Marketing und die Gestaltung der Kampagne ist Luise Bachmann, Heike Stumpf, Hannah Ruiz und Elena Schmidt zu verdanken. Johanna Pulz, Julia Bastian, Elisabeth Pallentin und Isabelle Hammer gilt mein Dank für die Pressearbeit. Antonia Lagemann möchte ich mit Anuschka Berthelius für die Koordination und Betreuung der Publikation sowie für die Redaktion des Schirn Magazins danken. Danken möchte ich für das begleitende Vermittlungsprogramm außerdem Chantal Eschenfelder mit Simone Boscheinen, Laura Heeg, Irmi Rauber und Olga Shmakova. Für die Entwicklung und Koordination der Veranstaltungen in der Schirn danke ich Ute Seiffert mit Lena Sobczinski; Julia Lange und Miriam Werner gilt mein Dank für das Sponsoring und die Betreuung der Partner und Förderer. Nicht zuletzt danke ich Heike Berndt, Claudia Kroh und Tanja Stahl in der Verwaltung der Schirn sowie Daniela Becker für die Assistenz in zahlreichen Belangen. Abschließend möchte ich dem Boten Stefan Schell und Lukas Müller, Rosaria La Tona und dem Team der Gebäudereinigung, Bettina Beyermann, Vilizara Antalavicheva und Josef Härig am Empfang sowie allen weiteren Mitarbeiterinnen und Mitarbeitern der Schirn danken, die an der Realisierung dieser einzigartigen Ausstellung und Publikation beteiligt waren.

Philipp Demandt
Direktor
Schirn Kunsthalle Frankfurt

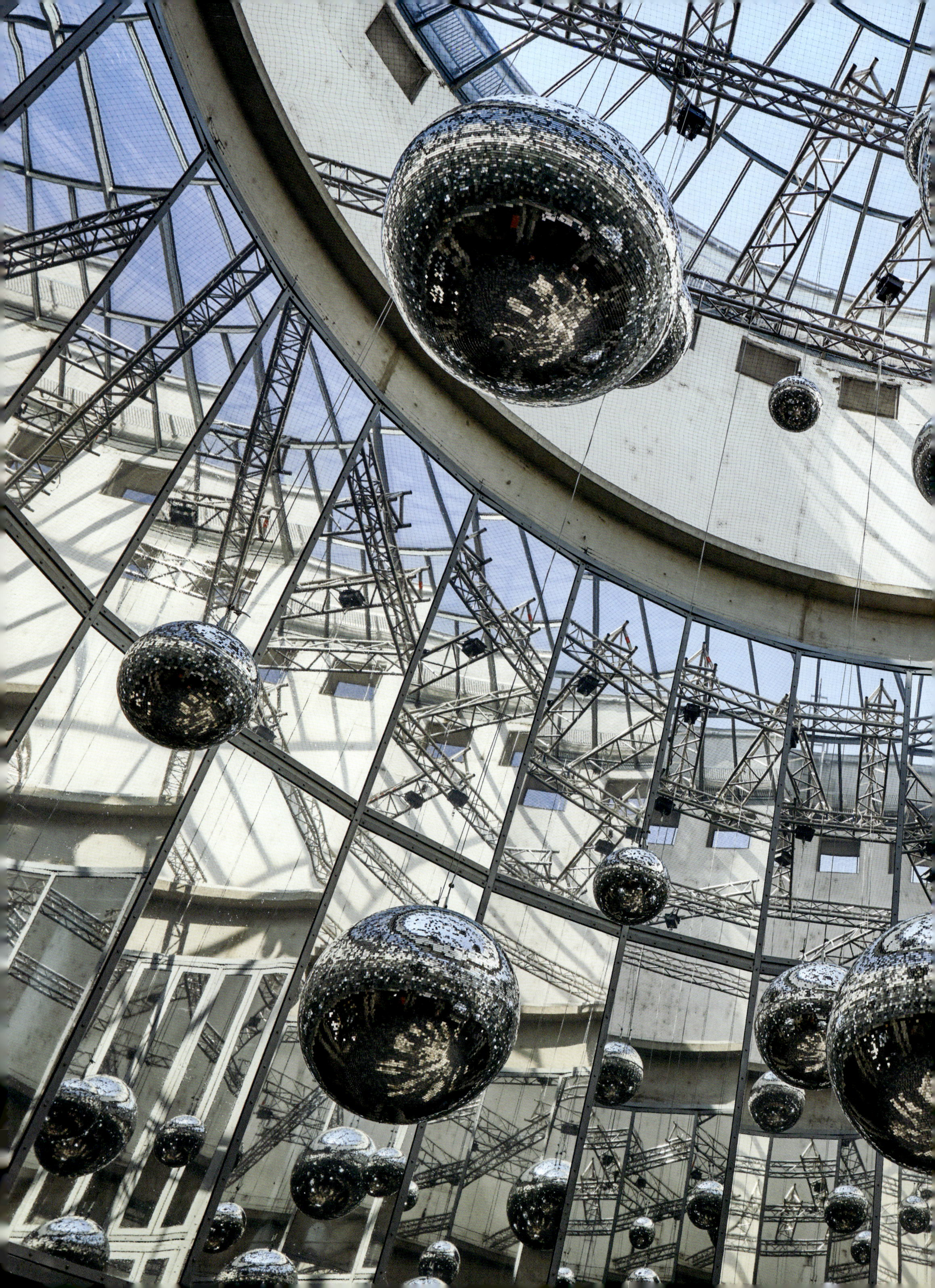

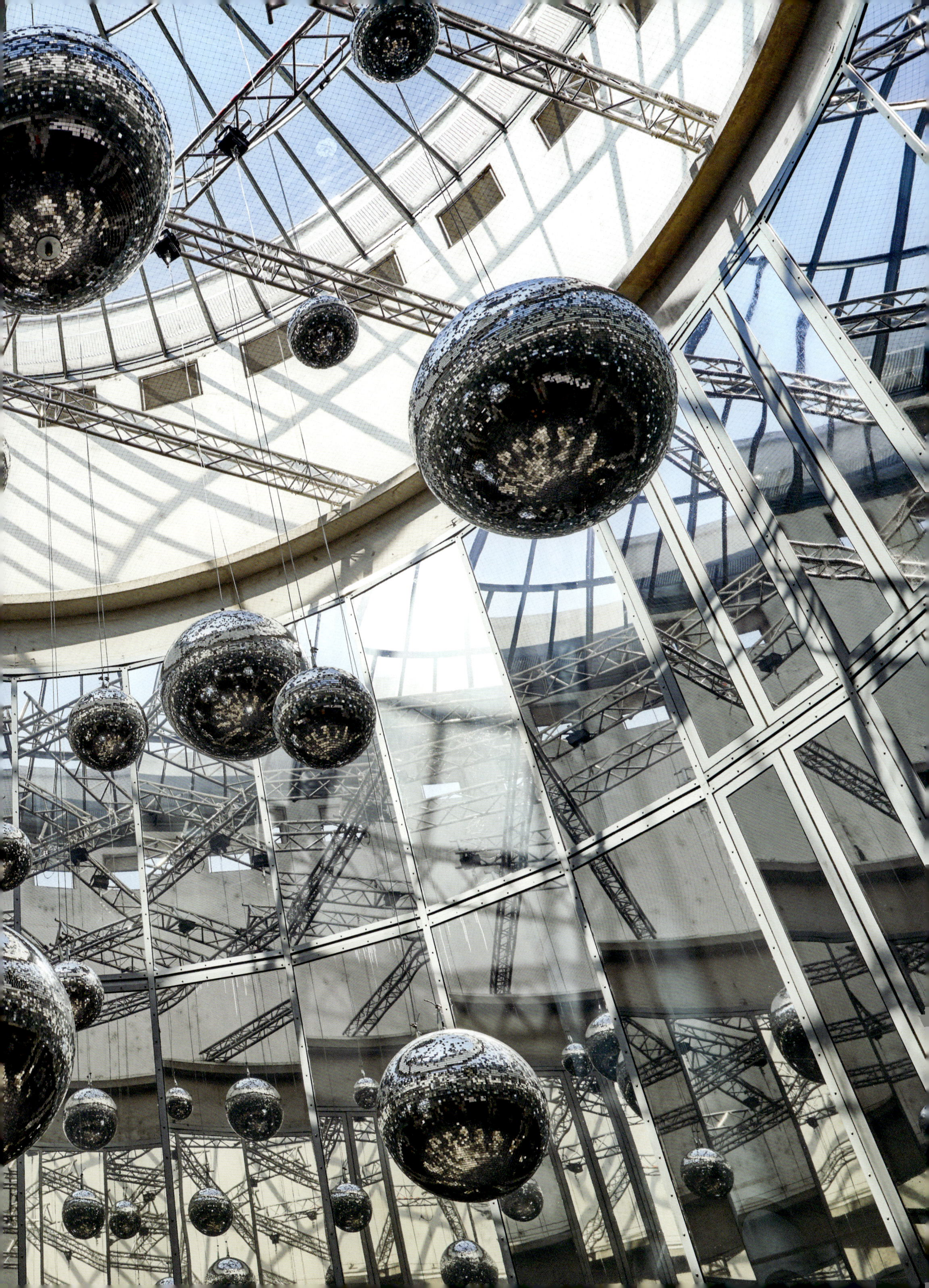

Zitat – Zufall – Ironie
John M Armleders Kunst der offenen Kommunikation

Ingrid Pfeiffer

»Die Freude an der Kunst bleibt für mich sehr rätselhaft, sowohl im Herstellen als auch im Betrachten.« John M Armleder, 1985[1]

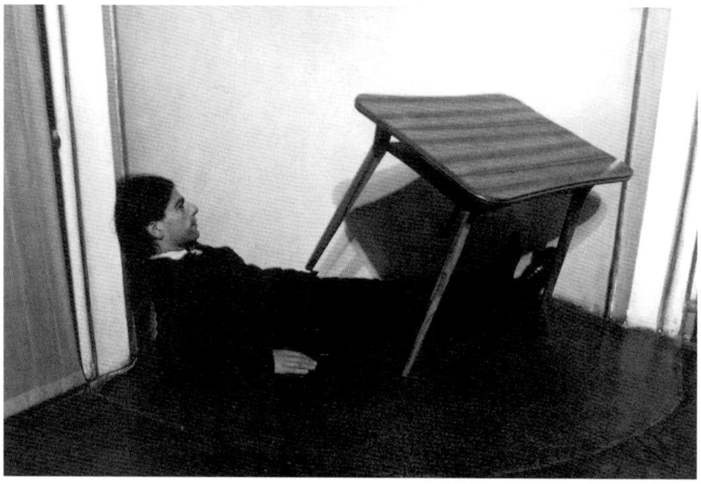

Abb. 1 John M Armleder mit *Furniture Sculpture* beim Kulturfestival *steirischer herbst '82* in Graz

1 Gespräch zwischen John M Armleder und Helmut Federle, Zürich 16./17.11.1985, in: *John M Armleder,* Ausst.-Kat. Wiener Secession 1993, S. 50.

Die Kunst von John M Armleder stellt uns als Betrachter vor Herausforderungen, die gar nicht zu ihrer lässigen Leichtigkeit zu passen scheinen. Seine Installationen voller Spiegel und Farben, Muster und Flächen, Discokugeln und Baugestänge, Pflanzen, ausgestopfter Tiere, alter Möbel, Monitore, Filme, Musik und sonstiger Versatzstücke unserer heutigen Welt lassen uns gleichermaßen fasziniert wie ratlos zurück. Elegant, perfekt inszeniert und leichtfüßig kommt das Werk Armleders daher, stimmig trotz aller Heterogenität – gleichzeitig wirkt es hermetisch und erschließt sich nicht ohne Weiteres. Treffen hier »Banalität und Komplexität« aufeinander, wie ein Kritiker einmal schrieb?[2]

»Meine Bilder sind völlig unvernünftig«, sagte Armleder dazu, »sie entziehen sich jeglichen intelligenten, diskursiven Verständnisses [...]. Was wir tun, hat nur wenig mit dem zu tun, was man glaubt, dass wir tun.«[3] Diese Aussage liegt schon viele Jahre zurück, doch die Strategie des Entziehens, Ausweichens und der Verschleierung findet sich in Armleders Praxis bis heute. Um tiefer einzudringen in die Grundlagen, die Voraussetzungen seiner Arbeit, müssen wir den Blick auf seine Anfänge richten, welche die Basis für alle späteren Arbeiten bildet.[4] Ins Auge springt, dass Armleder permanent die Kunstgeschichte zitiert, und hier besonders die abstrakt-geometrische Tradition und die Konzeptkunst. Farbige Flächen, Streifen, Ringe, Kreise oder andere geometrische Elemente in Armleders Arbeiten sind uns aus den Anfängen der Abstraktion der Klassischen Moderne vertraut – einem längst abgeschlossenen Kapitel der Kunstgeschichte, das uns heute vorkommt wie die »heroische« Zeit in der Kunst. Der Konstruktivismus oder Suprematismus feierte nicht nur neue formale Erfindungen – wie die Abstraktion –, sondern die Künstler glaubten an eine lebens- und gesellschaftsverändernde Kraft ihrer Werke. Ihre Texte waren oft Manifeste, ihre Kämpfe waren heldenhaft, ob gegen das aus ihrer Sicht Verstaubte, Antimoderne oder gegen massive politische Unterdrückung. Von Malewitsch bis Rothko ist die abstrakte und geometrische Kunst ohne ihre spirituelle Seite kaum zu denken – denn was wäre Malewitschs *Schwarzes Quadrat,* würde man nicht die ganz großen Fragen darin lesen, nach Raum und Zeit, nach dem »Endpunkt« der Malerei, oder sogar nach dem großen Nichts beziehungsweise der Göttlichkeit? Nicht umsonst wurden Malewitschs Farben mit der Palette der russischen Ikonenmalerei verglichen, und auch seine Texte bewegen sich auf einer Metaebene. Obwohl Armleder sich von dieser Form der Kunstbetrachtung sehr weit

2 Markus Brüderlin: »Ironie und Fundamentalismus. Vom Schicksal der abstrakten Kunst am Anfang der neunziger Jahre«, in: *John M Armleder,* Ausst.-Kat. Wiener Secession 1993, S. 39.

3 John M Armleder in einem Interview mit Christoph Schenker, in: *Flash Art,* 130, 1986, S. 68.

4 Friederike Nymphius: *John M Armleder. Pudding Overdose,* Heidelberg 2002, S. 7.

entfernt hat, sagt er: »Ich glaube, die historischen Avantgarden sind immer in meinem Kopf, was vielleicht nicht auf die jungen Künstler von heute zutrifft.«[5] Gemeinsam war den Künstlern immer der Glaube daran, dass es den »Fortschritt« gibt in der Kunst, dass jeder, der etwas Neues schafft, besser sein kann als die Vorgänger, dass Innovation immer auf Innovation folgen wird. Dieser Haltung hat Armleder schon lange eine Absage erteilt. »Ich mache nichts anderes, als das, was andere schon einmal gemacht haben«,[6] war seit den 1980er-Jahren sein Statement – doch es wird sich zeigen, dass auch das nur bedingt möglich ist und Armleder sehr wohl viele Dinge tut, die nur er tun kann.

Als Armleder Ende der 1960er-Jahre seine künstlerische Karriere begann, war nicht nur die Moderne längst vergangen, sondern auch die an die geometrische Tradition anknüpfende Minimal Art bereits am Ausklingen. Die Pop-Art hatte das künstlerische Wertesystem gründlich durcheinandergewirbelt. Selbst die Fluxus-Bewegung mit ihrer Suche nach einer ephemeren Kunst voller billiger Materialien und mit ihrer Absage an den Marktwert der Kunst befand sich bereits in ihrer späten Phase. Fluxus knüpfte mit anderen Mitteln an die Kunst der Moderne an: Ideales Ziel war auch hier wieder die engere Verbindung von »Kunst und Leben«. Mit Multiples, Performances und Gruppenaktivitäten erteilten die Fluxus-Künstler der individuellen Handschrift und dem einzelnen, wertvollen und teuren Kunstwerk eine Absage. Ideen sollten grundsätzlich wichtiger sein als »Dinge«.

Wesentlich jünger als andere Fluxus-Künstler wie John Cage, Alan Kaprow, Emmett Williams, Dick Higgins oder Ben Vautier, startete Armleder 1973 seine erste Ausstellung mit der Gruppe Ecart in Genf, die bereits 1969 gegründet worden war und für die er ein Manifest verfasst hatte: Ecart bedeutet im Französischen Abweichung – gemeint war eine Verweigerung des Konkreten, des Festlegbaren: Schon zu diesem Zeitpunkt waren Armleders Parameter zumindest in dieser Hinsicht definiert. Auch die eigenen oder fremden Ideen nochmals aufzugreifen und wiederzuverwerten, war in der Groupe Ecart gängige Praxis[7] und blieb es für Armleder auch weiterhin.

Eine seiner ersten Installationen war 1973 John Cage gewidmet (Abb. 2) – ein akustisches Sammelsurium aus zehn Audio-Stücken lebender und verstorbener Künstler, darunter die Fluxus-Künstler George Brecht und Dick Higgins, aber auch die »Urväter« des Dada wie Tristan Tzara, Kurt Schwitters und vor allem Marcel Duchamp. Die Auswahl der Künstler verweist auf Armleders

5 Helena Kontova und Giancarlo Politi, »John M Armleder. A Gentleman in the Fluxus Tradition« (Interview), in: *Flash Art*, 63, 1992, S. 64.

6 »Suzanne Pagé im Gespräch mit John Armleder«, in: *John M Armleder*, Ausst.-Kat. Winterthur 1987, S. 63.

7 Nymphius 2002 (wie Anm. 4), S. 16.

persönliche Vorlieben und Referenzen.[8] Das Spielerische, Offene, die Einbeziehung von Zufall, dem Subversiven und Ungeplanten sind wichtige Elemente für Armleders Kunstverständnis bis heute. Mit John Cage teilte der Künstler nicht nur das Interesse an Musik, sondern auch am Zen-Buddhismus, bei dem eine gewisse Passivität gewünscht ist und dem zufällig Unbestimmten Raum gelassen wird.[9] Wer Armleder kennt, ist nicht überrascht von solchen Vorlieben, denn loslassen, entspannt sein, die Dinge geschehen lassen, auch wenn das Ergebnis zuletzt ein ganz anderes ist, als geplant, oder sich erst im Prozess entwickelt – genau das charakterisiert seine Arbeitsweise.

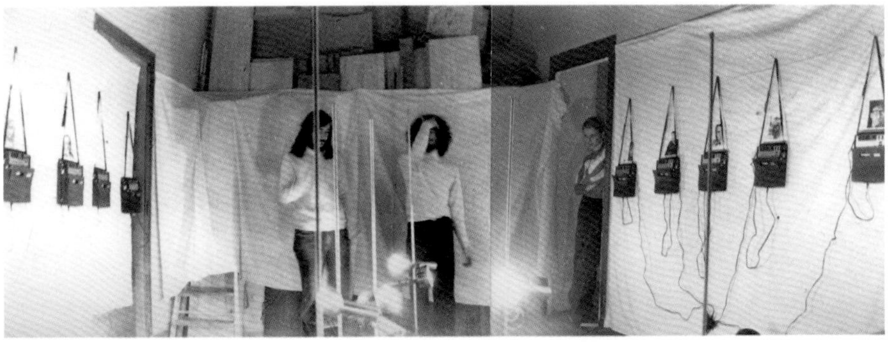

Abb. 2 John M Armleder
Conversation, Etude pour John Cage sur dix bandes magnétiques, 1973

Nach den Fluxus-Experimenten der 1970er-Jahre veränderte sich Armleders formales Vokabular und wurde dann besonders seit den 1990er-Jahren geradezu gegenläufig zu Fluxus: Statt »armer« Materialien dominieren bis heute farbig leuchtende, spiegelnde und scheinbar glamouröse Oberflächen, sodass diese Kombination mit der oben erwähnten Zen-Philosophie sogar als »Disco Zen« beschrieben wurde.[10] Doch die Performances, die Armleder bis heute durchführt, beruhen immer noch auf Grundprinzipien der Fluxus-Künstler: »[...] wir performten auch jahrelang die Skripte der Fluxus-Leute, und das mache ich tatsächlich immer noch.«[11]

Zu Armleders bekanntesten Werken zählen die ab 1979 entstandenen *Furniture Sculptures,* geometrische Malerei kombiniert mit gefundenen und benutzten Alltagsmöbeln oder auch Musikinstrumenten (Abb. 3). In diesen Arbeiten spiegelt sich Armleders Konzept der Kombinatorik, nicht nur von Medien (Malerei) und Dingen (Möbel), sondern auch in der Überlagerung von Zeichen und der Vermischung von Kontexten, da der Betrachter nun selbst

8 Ebd., S. 19.
9 Ebd., S. 24.
10 Alessandro Rabottini, »Disco Zen« (Interview), in: *John Armleder – Voltes IV,* Ausst.-Kat. Galleria d'arte moderna e contemporanea, Bergamo, Mailand 2004.
11 Henri Neuendorf, »John Armleder on Why Art Is more Important than Artists« (Interview), in: *artnet news,* 19.1.2017, https://news.artnet.com/art-world/john-armleder-interview-822530 (Zugriff 6.6.2019).

einen Teil der Interpretation zu leisten hat. Hier mischt sich erstmals High und Low, bekannte Formen der Kunstgeschichte mit Design, mit banalen Dingen des täglichen Gebrauchs. Armleder vermeidet bis in die Gegenwart solche Vergleiche und Bezüge nicht, sondern bezieht sie ein, im Bewusstsein, dass die Trivialkultur eine andere Form der Kommunikation mit dem Betrachter ermöglicht. Zumindest gibt es Wiedererkennungseffekte, die aber gleichzeitig ironisch gebrochen und ambivalent verfremdet werden. Armleder lockt sozusagen den Betrachter auf vertrautes Terrain, doch das Bekannte entpuppt sich als nur scheinbar, und jede Erkenntnis verwischt – der Künstler wahrt immer ironische Distanz. »Meine Arbeit wahrt eine gewisse Distanz, an der ich mich sehr erfreue«, sagt Armleder dazu.[12]

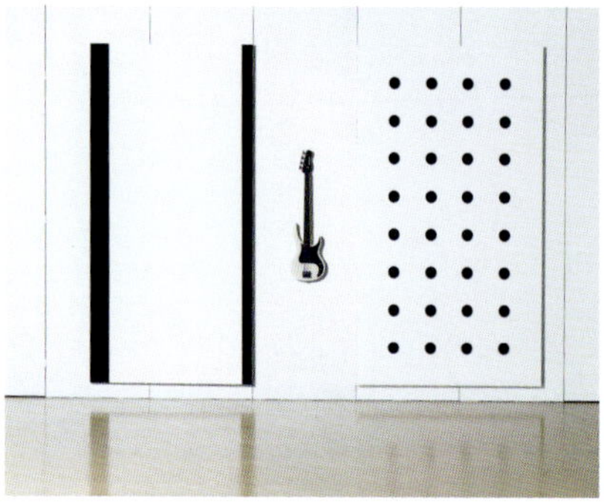

Abb. 3 John M Armleder
Furniture Sculpture 132, For the love of Daisy, 1986

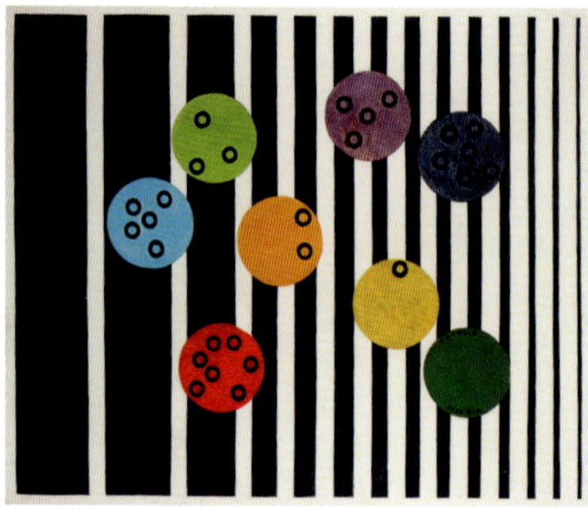

Abb. 4 Francis Picabia
Volucelle [II], 1923

Historisch reagierten die Künstler in Europa und den USA mit ihrer Rückkehr zur Geometrie auch auf die neue wilde, figurative Malerei der 1980er-Jahre. Armleder war durch seine Zeit in New York in Kontakt mit amerikanischen Neo-Geo-Künstlern wie Peter Halley, Haim Steinbach oder Jeff Koons, die Minimal mit Pop-Elementen kombinierten, ging aber als Europäer stärker von der europäischen Avantgarde-Tradition aus.

Während die *Furniture Sculptures* noch an klassische Bildformate anknüpften, also eine räumliche Begrenzung hatten und sich sozusagen nur nach vorne in den Raum ausdehnten, erweiterte Armleder die Formen und Muster soweit, dass die gesamte Wand, der gesamte Ausstellungsraum einbezogen wurde: »In gewisser Weise glaube ich an die totale Vermischung von Oberfläche und Inhalt.«[13] Armleder erläutert, dass dieser Prozess des »all-over« einsetzte, weil er und andere Künstler sich vom Zwang zur Komposition

12 Kontova / Politi 1992 (wie Anm. 5), S. 68.
13 Rabottini 2004 (wie Anm. 10), S. 38.

befreien wollten. Die häufig verwendeten Punkte und Streifen, regelmäßig oder nach dem Zufallsprinzip auf der Wand verteilt, finden ihre Vorläufer im Werk Francis Picabias, einem Künstler, dessen zahlreiche Stilwechsel und spielerische Ironie für Armleders Haltung Vorbild waren (Abb. 4). »Ich bin so eine Art Picabia, der eine andersartige Sache nach der anderen machte und der niemals aufgehört hat, andersartige Sachen zu machen«, beschreibt Armleder seinen Arbeitsprozess.[14]

Die Zufälligkeit im Ergebnis ist das Hauptmerkmal von Armleders *Pour Paintings* (Abb. S. 30/31), großformatigen Schüttbildern, in denen sich jedes Kompositionsprinzip auflöst. Unterschiedliche – billige, teure und zum Teil nicht kompatible – Materialien werden vermischt, zusammengeschüttet und erzeugen ein Ergebnis, das bleibt, wie es ist. Der Künstler akzeptiert es als Teil des Prozesses. »Ich bin ein totaler Fan des Zufalls«, sagt Armleder dazu. »Der Zufall bringt uns das Paradies. Der große Zufall liquidiert jeden Totalitarismus. Er ist der große Gleichmacher und ein einziges Entzücken.«[15]

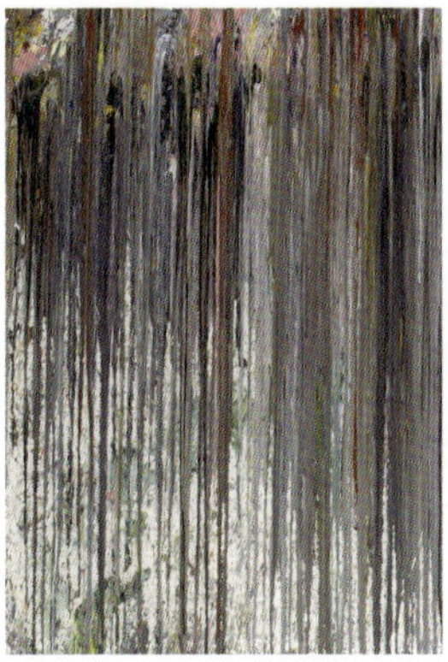

Abb. 5 Larry Poons *Untitled (18-A)*, 1976

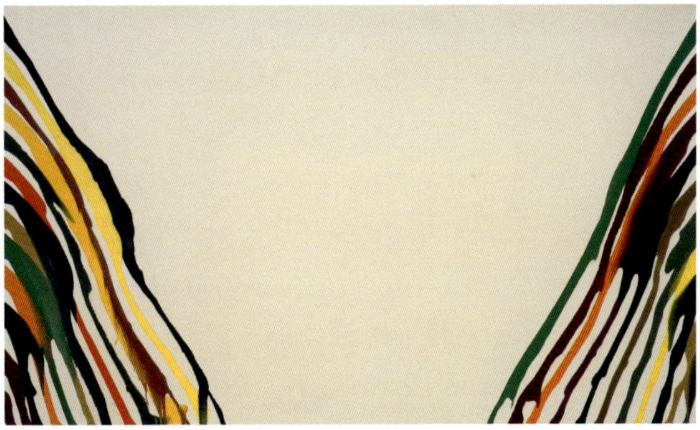

Abb. 6 Morris Louis *Beta Zeta*, 1960/61

Als einen Vorläufer dieser Schüttbilder nennt Armleder den weitgehend unbekannten amerikanischen Maler Larry Poons (Abb. 5), der sich in den 1970er-Jahren wiederum auf Morris Louis (Abb. 6) aus den frühen 1960er-Jahren bezogen hat. Ein solches ständiges »Recycling« von Formen – auch »Refocusing« genannt[16] – nimmt in Armleders Konzept eine zentrale Rolle ein, denn er befragt permanent die heutige Rolle der Kunst in einem unwiederbringlich veränderten und sich ständig weiter verändernden Kultursystem. Wie viele andere Künstler musste Armleder in den 1980er-Jahren den damals

14 Neuendorf 2017 (wie Anm. 11).
15 Gespräch zwischen John M Armleder und Raphaela Platow im Oktober 2006, in: *John M Armleder. Too Much is Not Enough*, Ausst.-Kat. Kunstverein Hannover, Heidelberg 2006, S. 103.
16 Nymphius 2002 (wie Anm. 4), S. 30.

überall erkennbaren »Erschöpfungszuständen der Moderne«[17] mit neuen Strategien begegnen.

Nicht umsonst verwendet Armleder gerne Spiegel und Plexiglas, Discokugeln und Leuchtstoffröhren in seinen Installationen. Was wir sehen, sind wir selbst oder ein Irrlicht der Wirklichkeit, gebrochen durch reflektierende Oberflächen, denn »die Wirklichkeit« gibt es ja laut Armleder gar nicht. Der Künstler empfindet vieles als relativ – ohne das wirklich zynisch zu meinen. In einem Interview mit seinem Künstlerfreund Helmut Federle beschreibt Armleder den eigenen Eklektizismus von Formen und Mitteln und seine »stille Offenlegung aller dieser Widersprüche«.[18]

Armleder kombiniert und konfrontiert viel Heterogenes – geometrische Formen versus geschüttete Bilder, Objets trouvés in der Tradition Marcel Duchamps mit Versatzstücken aus Mode, Musik und Alltag. »Ich mischte gewissermaßen alles zusammen«, sagt Armleder.[19] Er hat Trends geprägt, und viele junge Künstler beziehen sich bis heute auf ihn als Einflussgeber. Im Gegensatz zu seinen jüngeren Nachfolgern kennt Armleder aber noch den Ursprung und die Bedeutung dessen, was er zitiert und ist insofern weit entfernt von einem Kunstverständnis, für das die Kunstgeschichte nur ein Steinbruch ist, aus dem wahllos das Nötige herausgebrochen wird. Armleder reflektiert zwar diese Entwicklung des »anything goes«, die in den 1980er-Jahren einsetzte und bis heute anhält – doch auch wenn er dies scheinbar wertfrei tut (oder versucht), so ist er doch Teil einer Generation, die durchaus noch den Verlust der Utopie schmerzhaft empfunden hat. Eine gewisse Melancholie blitzt immer durch, wenn Armleder über die Kunst der Vergangenheit spricht, die er zitiert, umformt und in etwas anderes, immer Neues verwandelt. »[...] auch wenn man denselben Stift verwendet, so schreibt man deshalb noch lange nicht denselben Text«, sagt Armleder. »Selbst dann nicht, wenn man dieselben Worte benützt oder dasselbe Papier. Es ist ein neuer Tag und ein anderer Planet [...]«[20]

Der Künstler glaubt, dass das wichtigste Element in der Dreierbeziehung zwischen Werk, Ort und Betrachter liegt – erst in dieser Kombination entwickelt sich die spezifische Bedeutung, deshalb entstehen viele Installationen vor Ort. »Ich definiere mein Werk nicht. Es funktioniert jedes Mal anders, für jeden einzelnen Betrachter, und so verbinden sich verschiedene Ebenen der Wahrnehmung. Ich mag noch immer die Idee von der Arbeit als Event.«[21]

17 Markus Brüderlin: »Das geflügelte Bild oder Malerei als Wiederholung. Iterativismus in der Abstraktion«, in: *Kunstforum International*, 105, 1990, S. 110–126.
18 Armleder / Federle 1993 (wie Anm. 1) S. 49.
19 Kontova / Politi 1992 (wie Anm. 5), S. 64.
20 »John Armleder: At Any Speed, ein Gespräch«, in: *Parkett*, 50, 1997, S. 40.
21 Rabottini 2004 (wie Anm. 10), S. 38.

Der Event, den Armleder in der Schirn umsetzt, heißt *CA.CA.* und besteht aus zwei Räumen, die zwar sehr unterschiedlich sind, jedoch zusammen viele Themen Armleders enthalten: In der Rotunde, dem Eingangsbereich der Schirn, hat der Künstler 20 unterschiedlich große, in mehreren Etagen hängende und sich langsam drehende Discokugeln befestigen lassen, die sich in den mit Spiegelfolie beklebten Fenstern spiegeln. Die Arbeit ist optisch überwältigend und passt sich perfekt den räumlichen Gegebenheiten an. In ihrer Mischung aus Glanz und billigem Dekor enthält sie das spielerische Element, das für Armleders Konzept charakteristisch ist. Im zweiten großen Raum der Schirn, der eine neue Installation enthält, zeigt Armleder sowohl seine bekannten *Pour Paintings* als auch speziell an den Ort angepasste Wandarbeiten. Wie immer hat er sich kurz vor Ausstellungsbeginn und unter Mitwirkung aller Beteiligten spontan an den örtlichen Gegebenheiten orientiert. Über 400 stilisierte Totenköpfe in Silber, Gold und Elfenbein – ein Motiv, das er schon häufiger für Wandmalereien im Tapetenstil eingesetzt hat – bedecken in unterschiedlichen Größen die Wände. So konsequent und raumfüllend hat Armleder dieses Vanitas-Motiv noch nie eingesetzt, das im Werk der meisten großen Künstler der Moderne – von Picasso bis Andy Warhol – zu finden ist. Auch hier treffen Banalität und Komplexität aufeinander und ergeben den für Armleder charakteristischen, sich vielfach überlagernden Mix aus Kontext und Bedeutung. Unter den Skulpturen, die an der Wand montiert werden und zu den früheren *Furniture Sculptures* gezählt werden können, ist eine auf dem Kopf stehende doppelte Kinderrutsche – Symbol für unsere von infantilem Größenwahn geprägte Gegenwart. Armleder selbst vermeidet solche Deutungen stets, ist aber äußerst tolerant, wenn wir als Betrachter darauf verfallen.

Armleders Kunst ist eine Herausforderung, eine konzeptuelle Tour de Force durch die Kunstgeschichte des 20. und 21. Jahrhunderts mit ihren Entwicklungen und gedanklichen Konsequenzen. Sie ist besonders zeitgemäß, weil sie ihre Quellen zwar verschleiert, aber nicht verleugnet. Sie ist einzigartig, obwohl und gerade weil der Künstler herkömmliche Innnovationen ablehnt. Es ist eine leichtfüßig daherkommende, verführerische Form der Konzeptkunst, die nicht nur das Auge und die Sinne befriedigt, sondern – wenn man sich darauf einlässt – auch den kritischen Geist.

Biografie
John M Armleder

Rebecca Herlemann

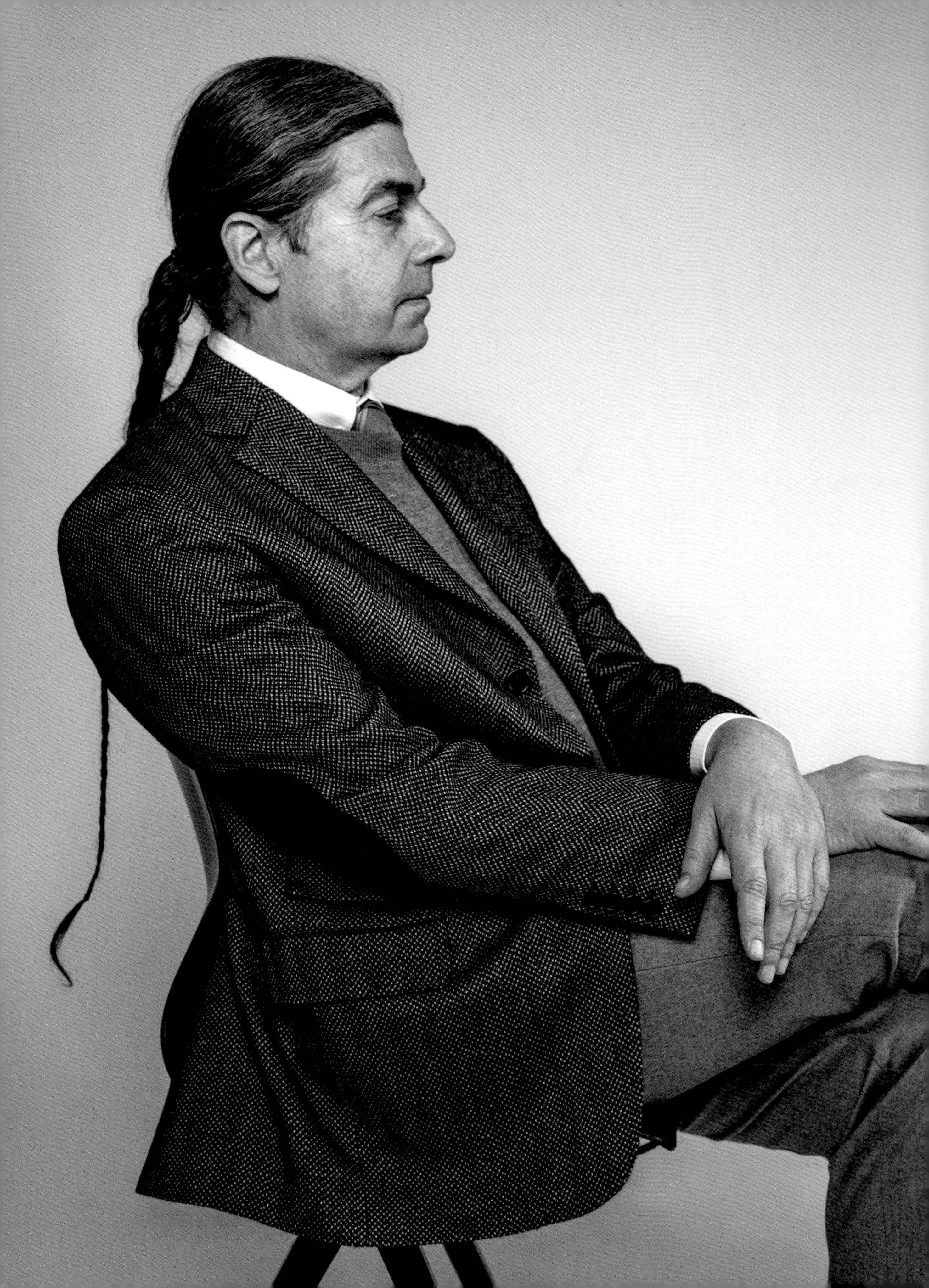

1948	John Michael Armleder wird am 24. Juni 1948 in Genf geboren.
Ab 1963	Musikalische und andere Aktivitäten mit der Groupe Luc Bois und der Groupe Max Bolli, Genf
1966/67	Studium an der Ecole des Beaux-Arts in Genf (ein Semester in der Abteilung Malerei, ein Semester in verschiedenen Ateliers)
1969	Teilnahme am Mixed Media Course *The Black Box* bei John Epstein an der Glamorgan Summer School, England Gründung der Groupe Ecart mit Patrick Lucchini und Claude Rychner. »Ecart« bedeutet auf Französisch Abweichung – gemeint ist eine Verweigerung des Konkreten, Festlegbaren. Die Gruppe organisiert Ausstellungen, Performances, Konzerte oder auch Konferenzen.
1972	Armleder gründet das Verlagshaus Ecart Publications. Veröffentlichungen von Werken von Mitgliedern der Groupe Ecart sowie von Peter Downsbrough, Robert Filliou, Dan Graham, Genesis P-Orridge, Sarkis, Endre Tót, Lawrence Weiner und anderen
1973	Gründung der Galerie Ecart, Rue Plantamour 6, Genf (ab 1979 zusammen mit dem Centre d'art contemporain an der Rue d'Italie 16). Ausstellungen von Mitgliedern der Groupe Ecart sowie von Joseph Beuys, John Cage, Giuseppe Chiari, Braco Dimitrijevic, Dick Higgins, George Maciunas, Olivier Mosset, Daniel Spoerri, Ben Vautier, Jan Voss, Andy Warhol und anderen
1974	Gründung der Ecart Performance Groupe
1975	Eröffnung der Buchhandlung Ecart / Books als Teil der Galerie, ab 1980 mit Fluxkiosk
1976	Mitbegründer des International Institutions Register (I.I.R.), dessen Ziel es ist, eine Liste von »künstlerisch initiierten Gegeninstitutionen« zu erstellen.
1977	Gründung der Leathern Wing Scribble Press; Mitbegründer der Künstlerkooperative Laboratorio, Mailand; Gründungsmitglied und Representative Director für Europa von Associated Art Publishers (der mobile Sitz der Vereinigung befindet sich in den USA)
1977–1979	Eidgenössisches Kunststipendium
1979	Es entstehen erste *Furniture Sculptures,* geometrische Malerei kombiniert mit gefundenen und benutzten Alltagsmöbeln und auch Musikinstrumenten.
Ab 1980	Teilnahme von Ecart an der Kunstmesse Art Basel mit eigenem Stand, an dem im täglichen Wechsel verschiedene Künstler präsentiert werden
Ab 1981	Armleder organisiert im eigenen Atelier in den Halles de l'Ile Ausstellungen von Alison Knowles, Peter Suter und Ben Vautier.

1984 Erste Einzelausstellung in der John Gibson Gallery, New York; zahlreiche weitere Ausstellungen folgen
Organisation der Ausstellung *Peinture abstraite,* Ecart, Genf, mit eigenen Werken sowie Arbeiten von Helmut Federle, Lucio Fontana, Sol LeWitt, Verena Loewensberg, Robert Mangold, Gerhard Merz, Olivier Mosset, Robert Motherwell, Blinky Palermo, Gerwald Rockenschaub, Robert Ryman, Jean-Frédéric Schnyder, Otto Zitko

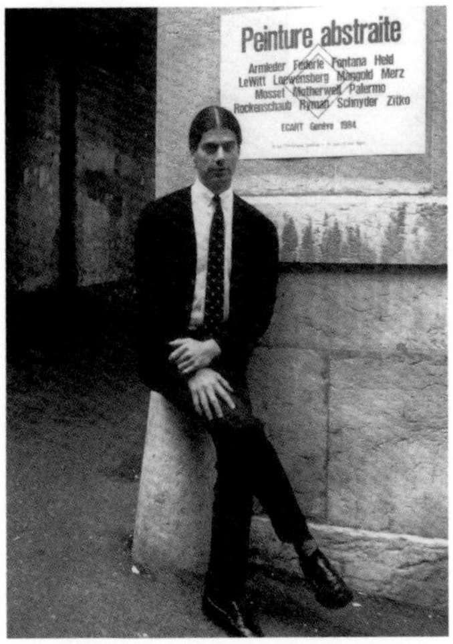

John M Armleder
Ausstellung *Peinture abstraite,* Genf 1984

1986 John M Armleder gestaltet den Schweizer Pavillon auf der 42. Biennale di Venezia.

Ab 1987 Edition von Multiples von Olivier Mosset und anderen Künstlern
Große Einzelausstellung im Kunstmuseum Winterthur / L'Arc Musée d'Art Moderne de la Ville de Paris / Kunstverein für die Rheinlande und Westfalen, Düsseldorf / Nationalgalerie Berlin
Teilnahme an der *Documenta 8,* Museum Fridericianum & Orangerie, Kassel

Ab 1989 Zweites Studio in New York, mit häufigen Aufenthalten dort

1992–2000 Mitglied der Eidgenössischen Kommission für bildende Künste, Bern

1993 Einzelausstellung in der Wiener Secession

1995–2013 Professor an der HBK Hochschule für Bildende Künste Braunschweig und der ECAL – Ecole cantonale d'art de Lausanne

1997 Gruppenausstellung *Ecart 1967–1982* im Musée d'Art Moderne et Contemporain, Genf

1999 Einzelausstellung *at any speed* in der Kunsthalle Baden-Baden

2018 Anlässlich Armleders 70. Geburtstag finden mehrere Retrospektiven statt, so im Museion, Bozen, und im Madre, Neapel.

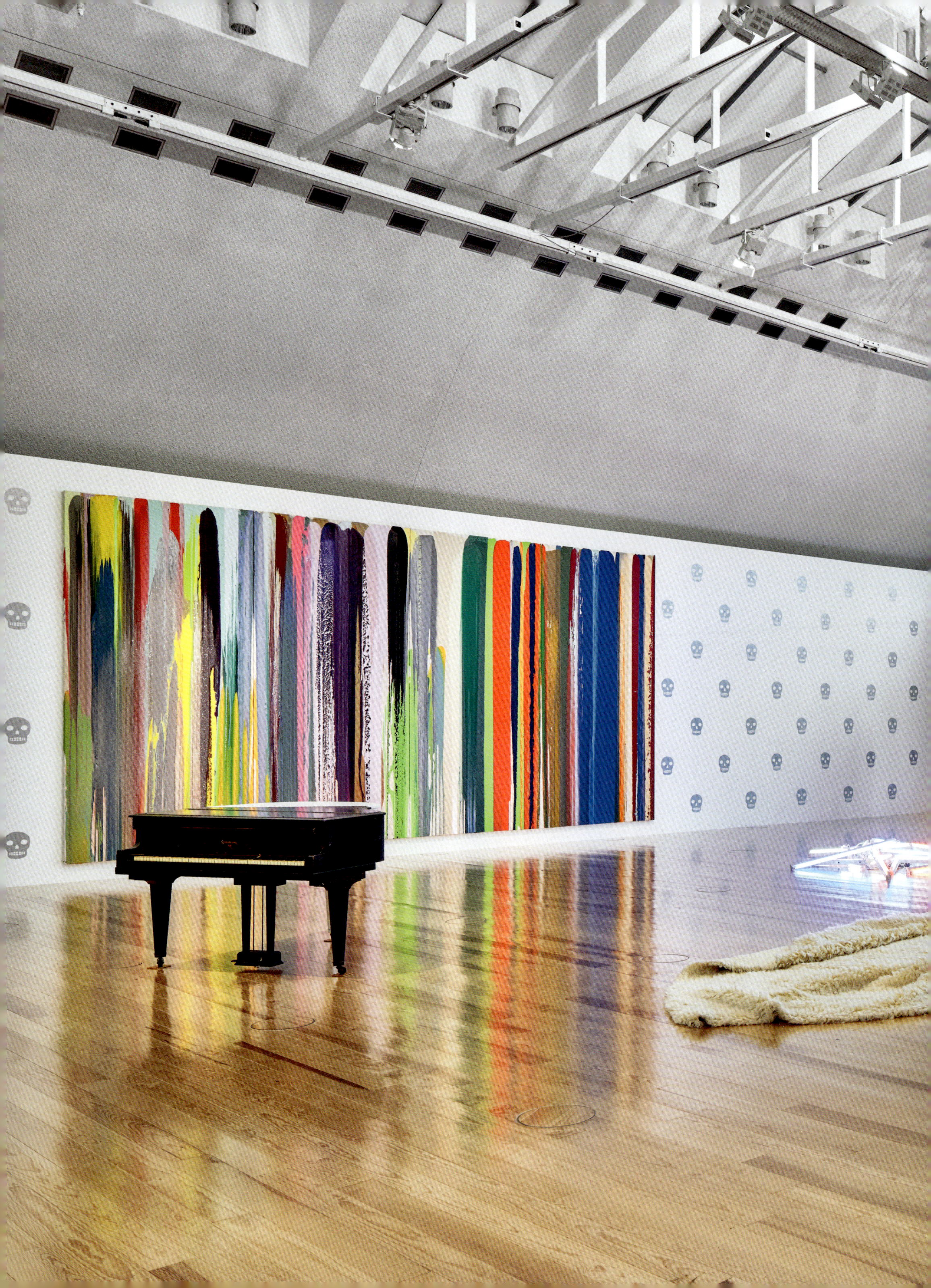

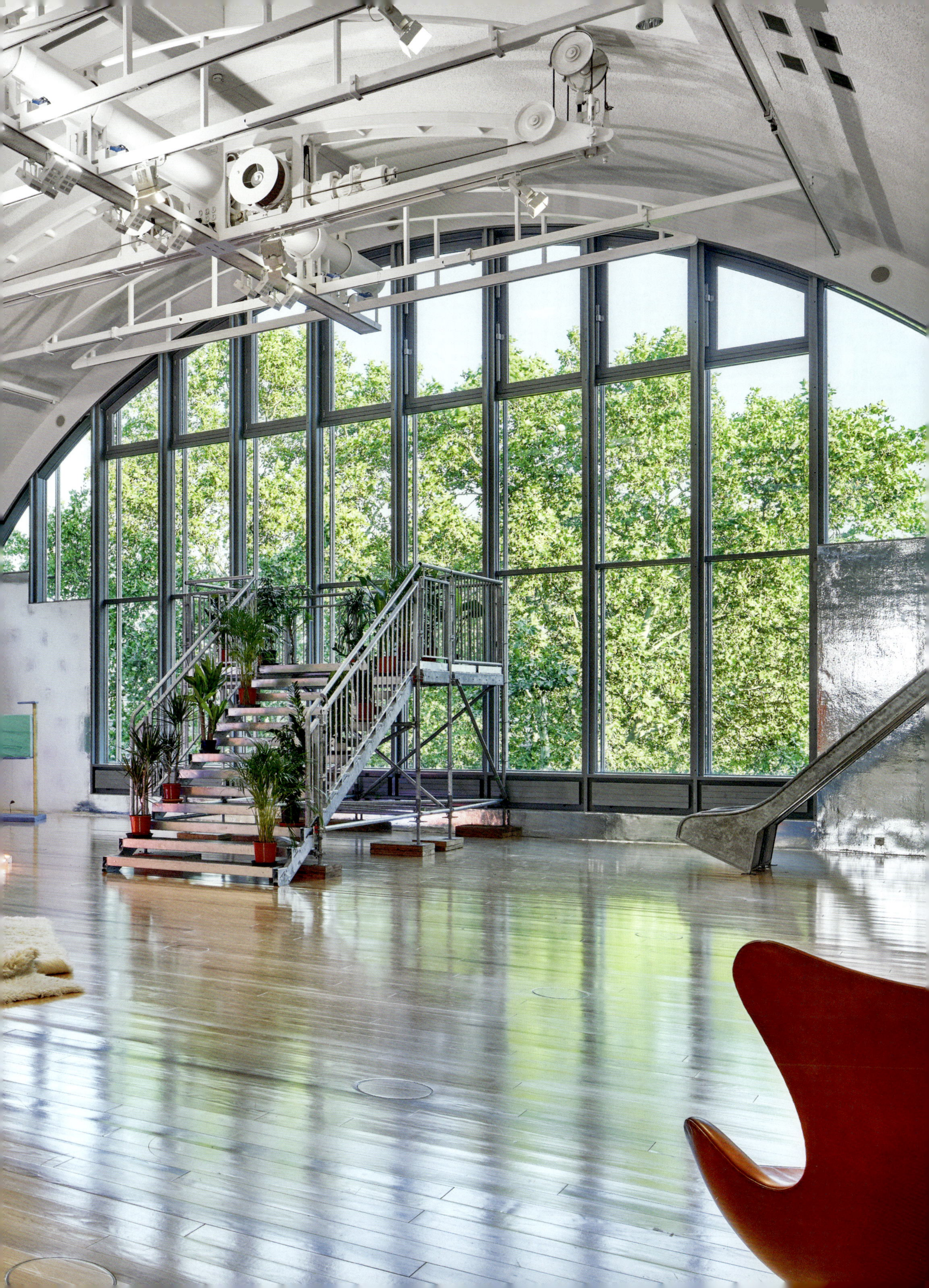

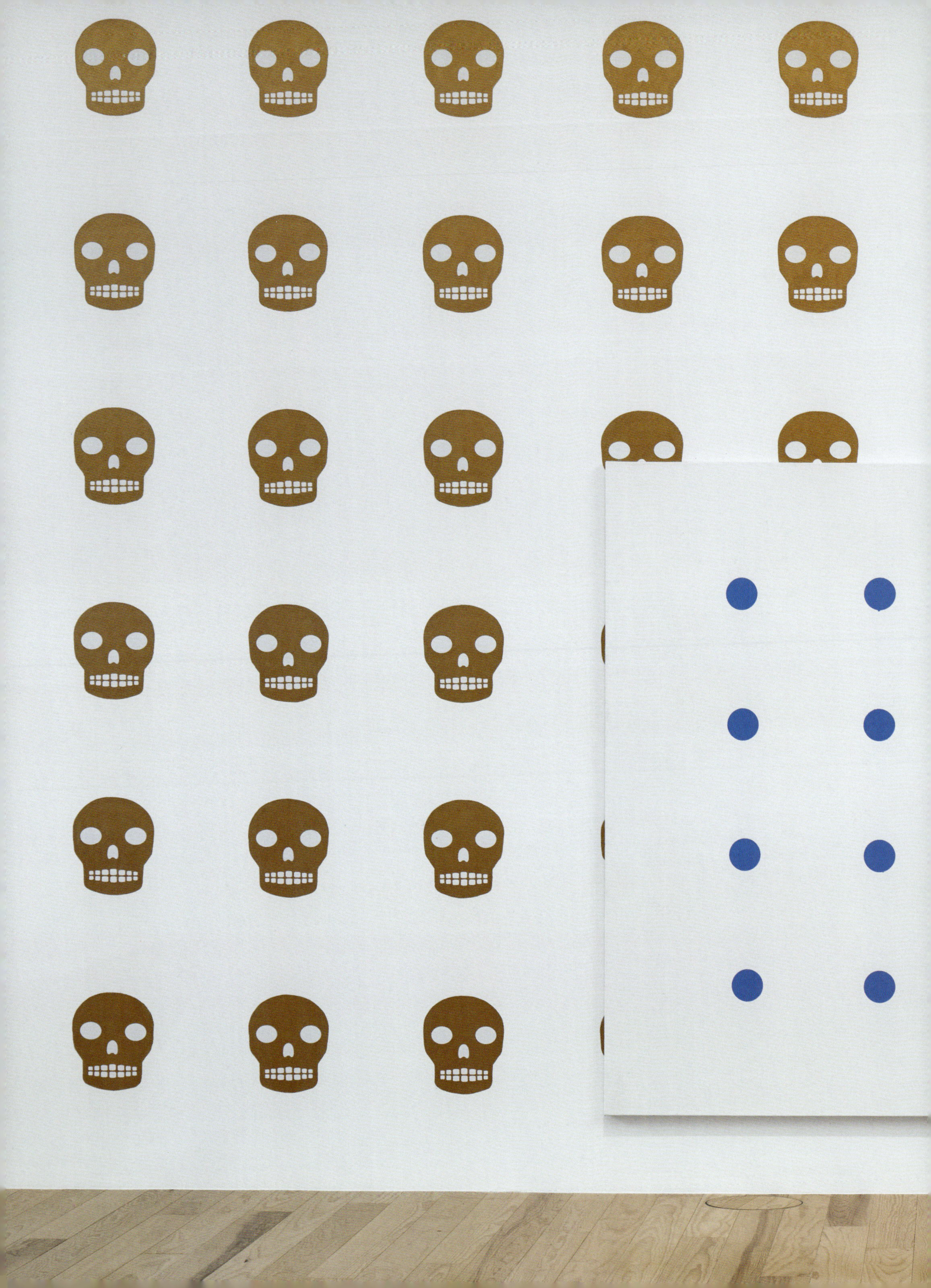

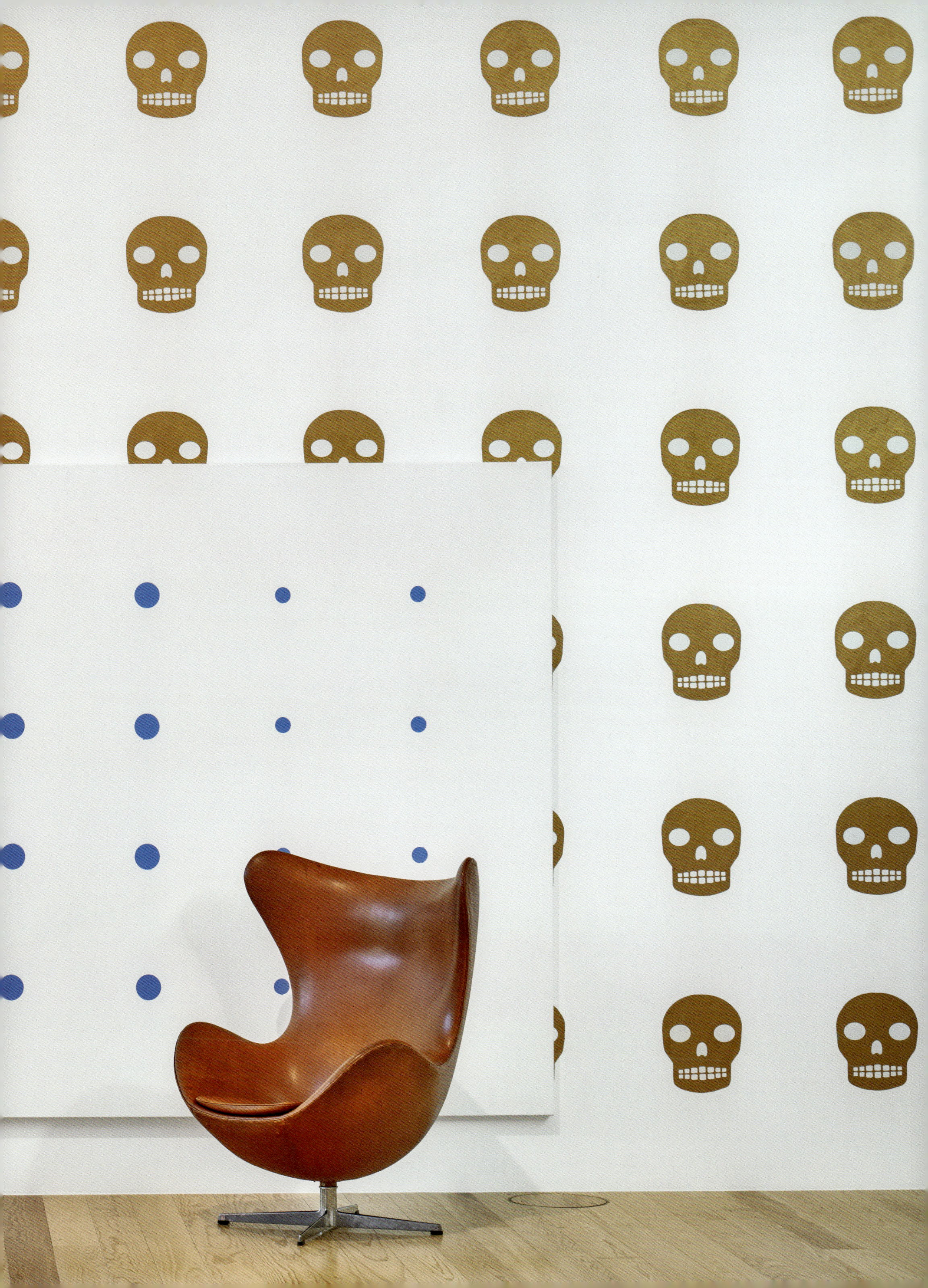

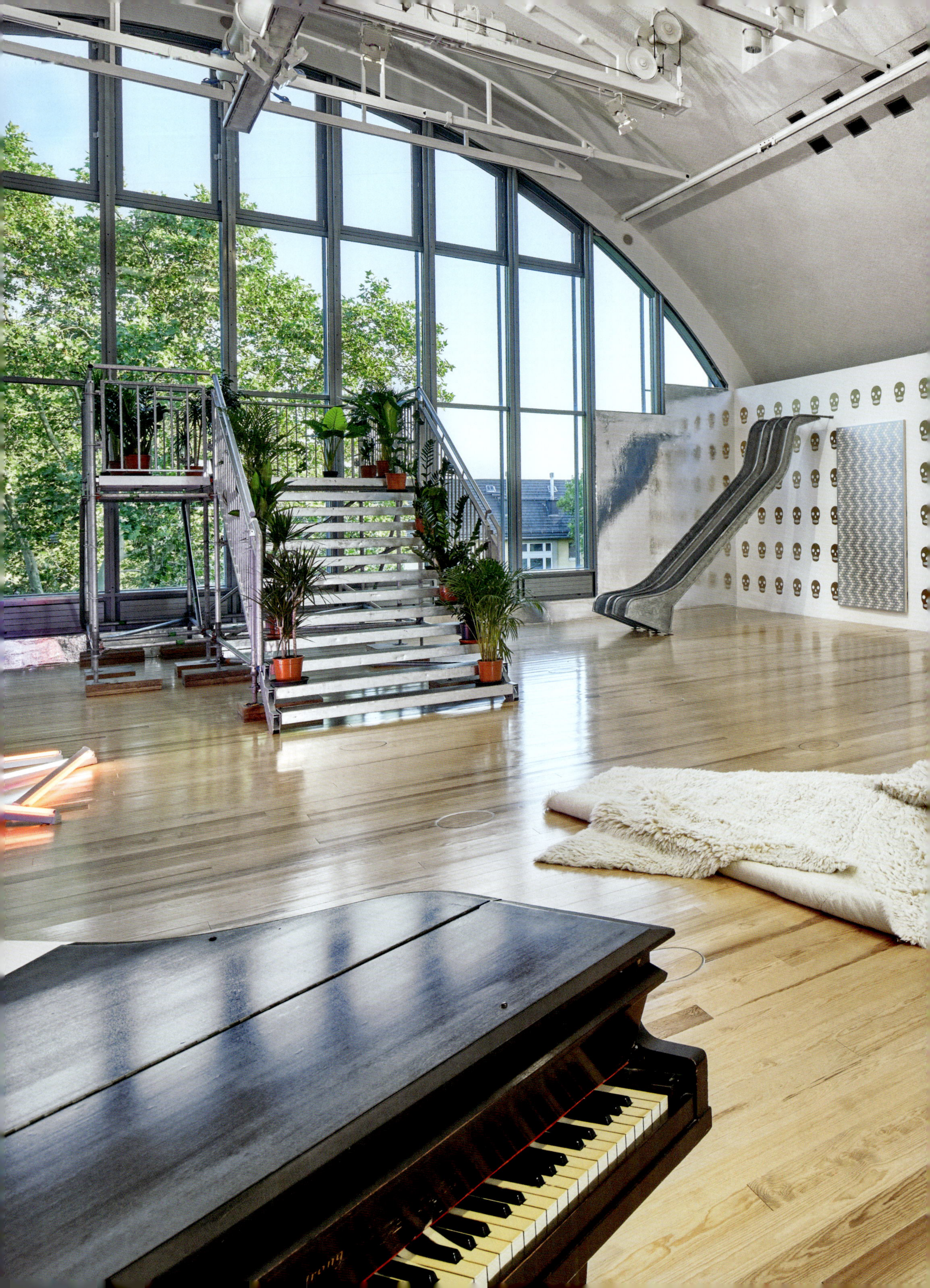

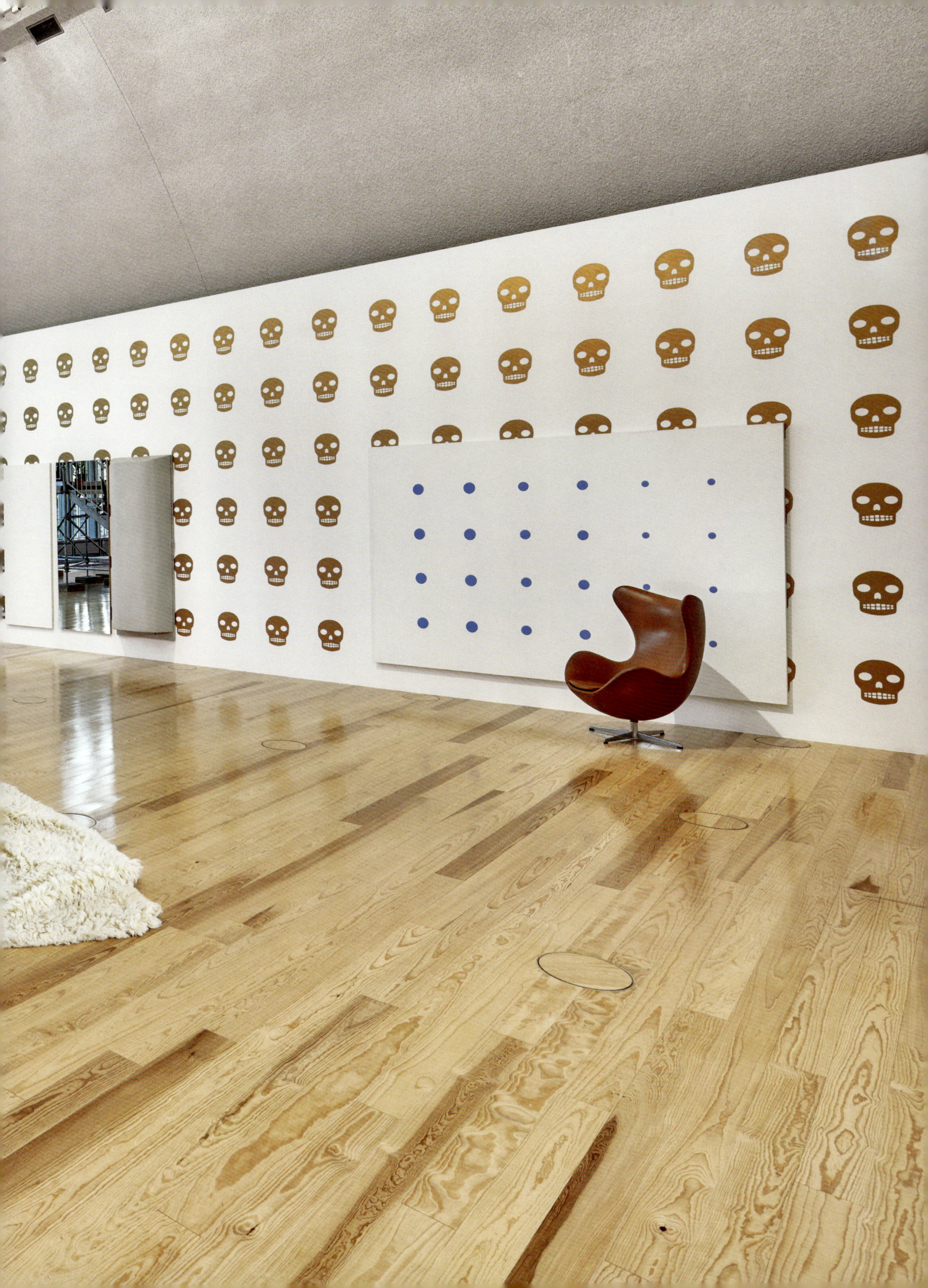

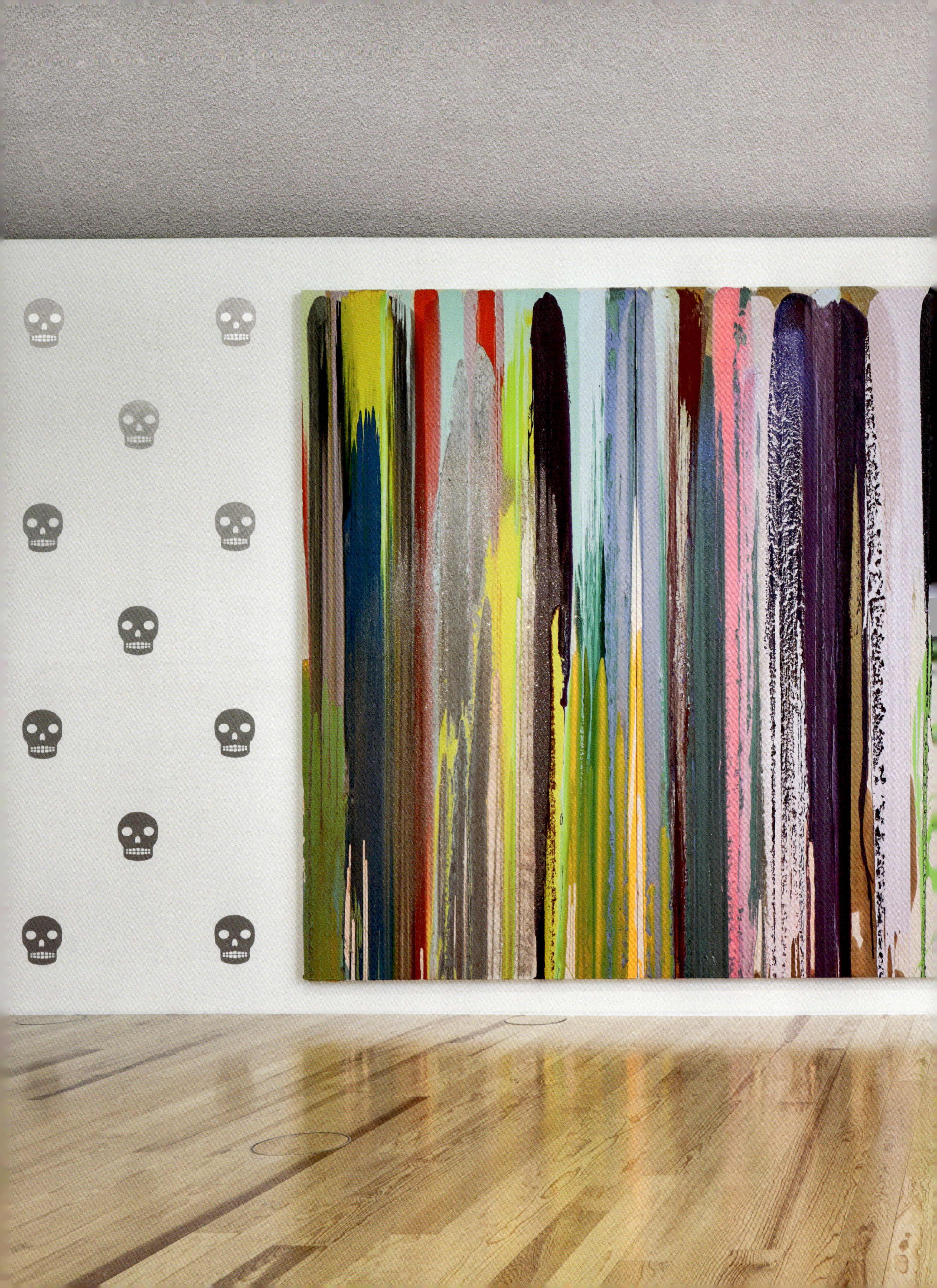

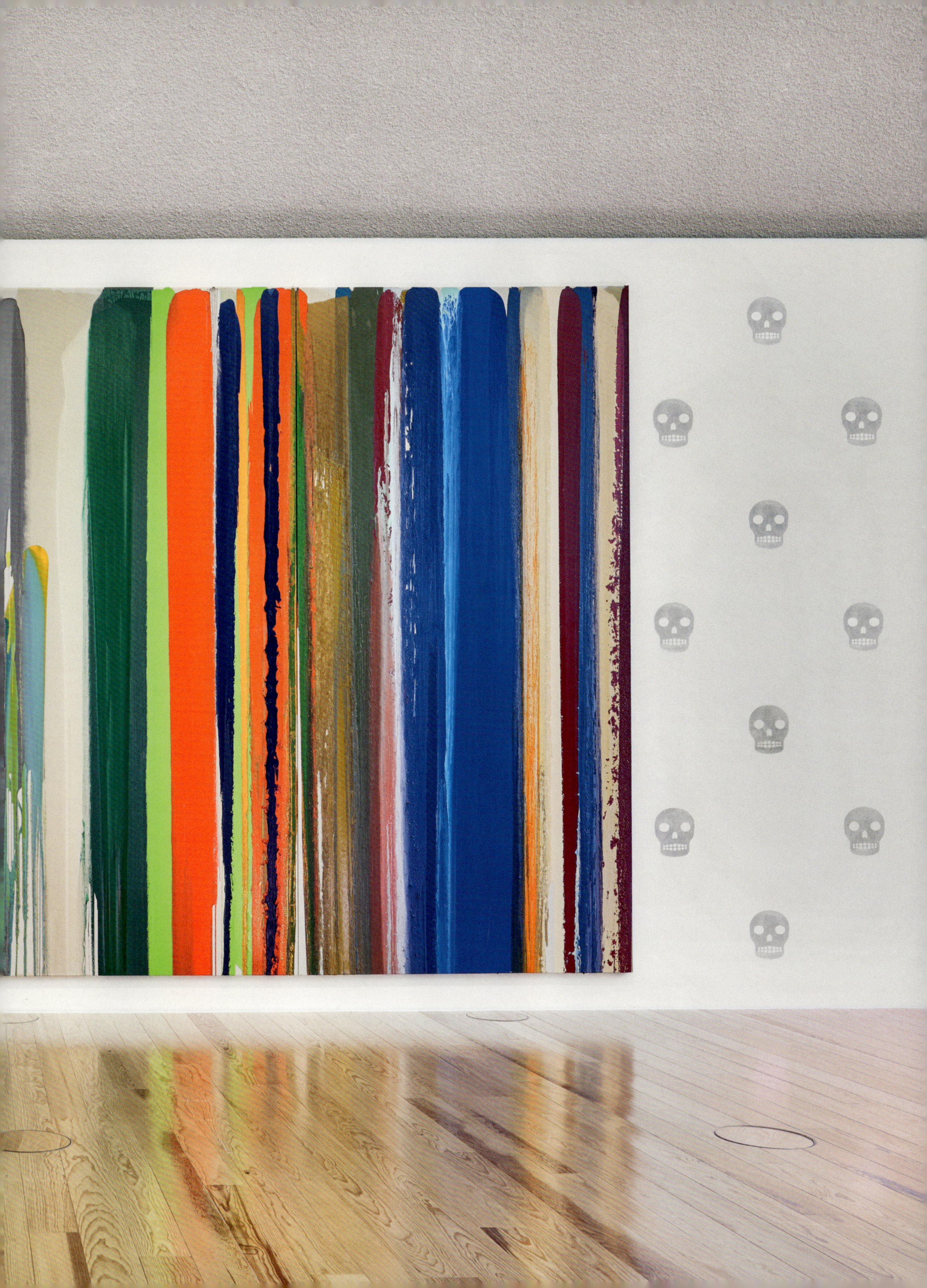

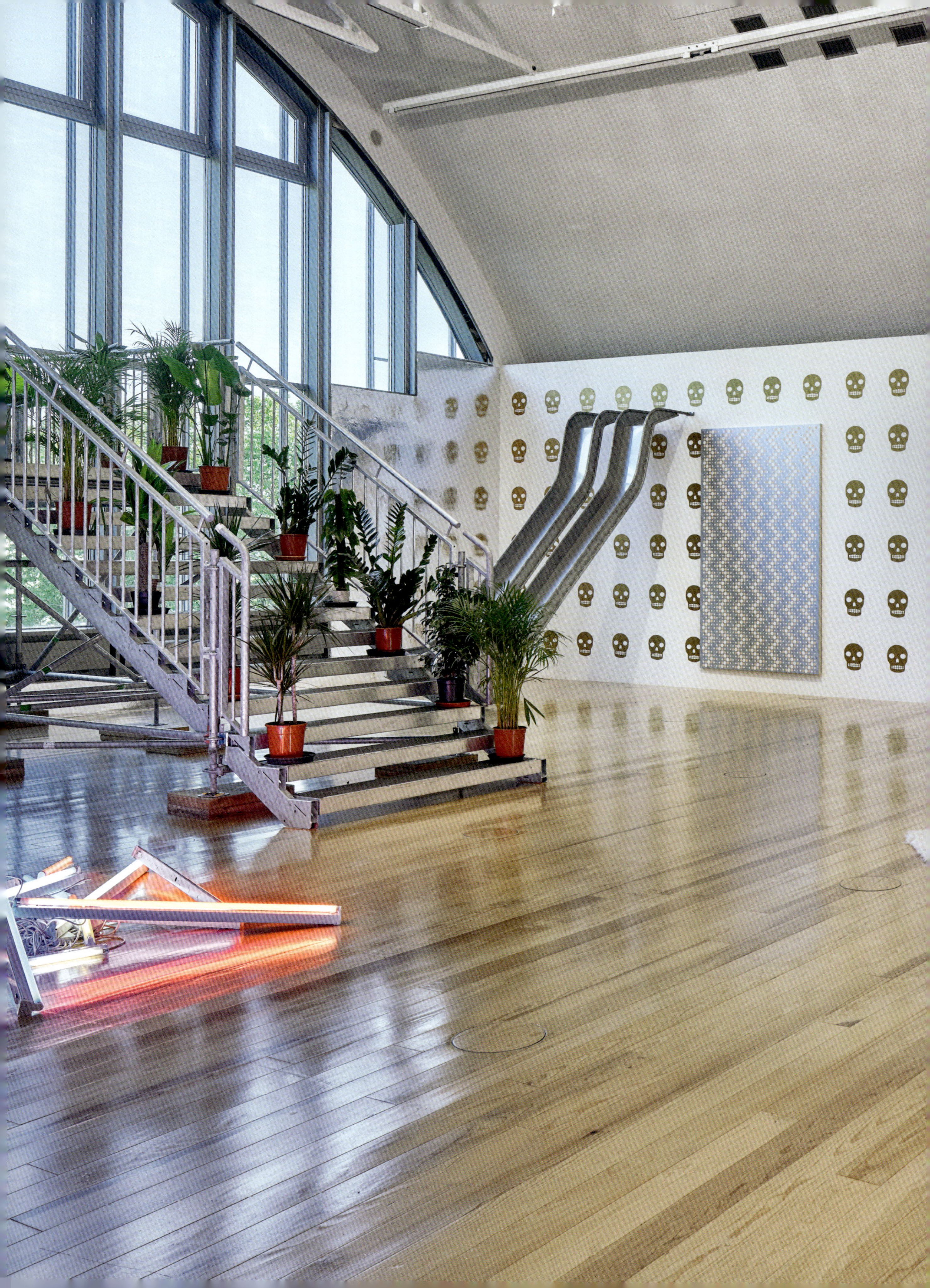

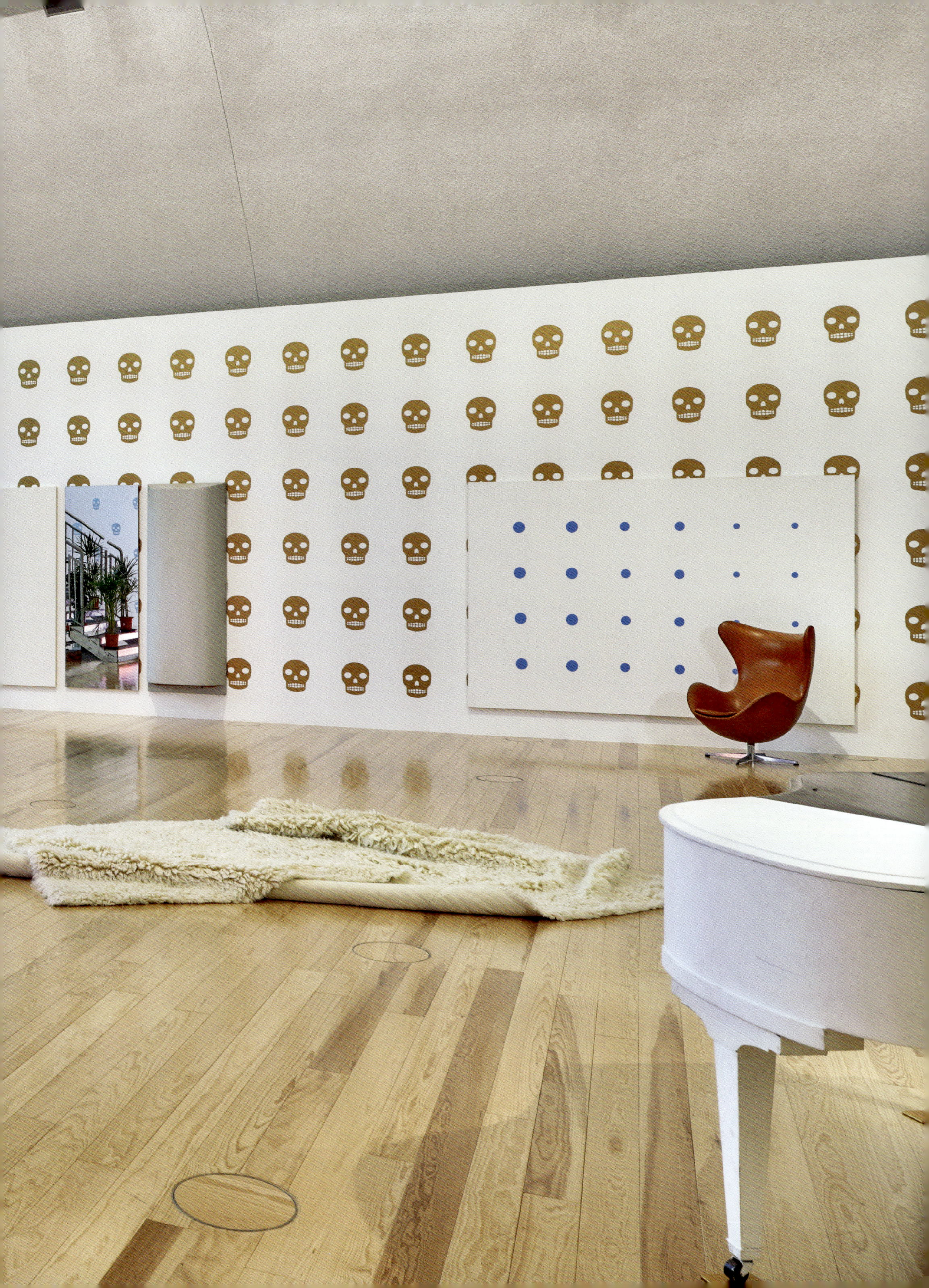

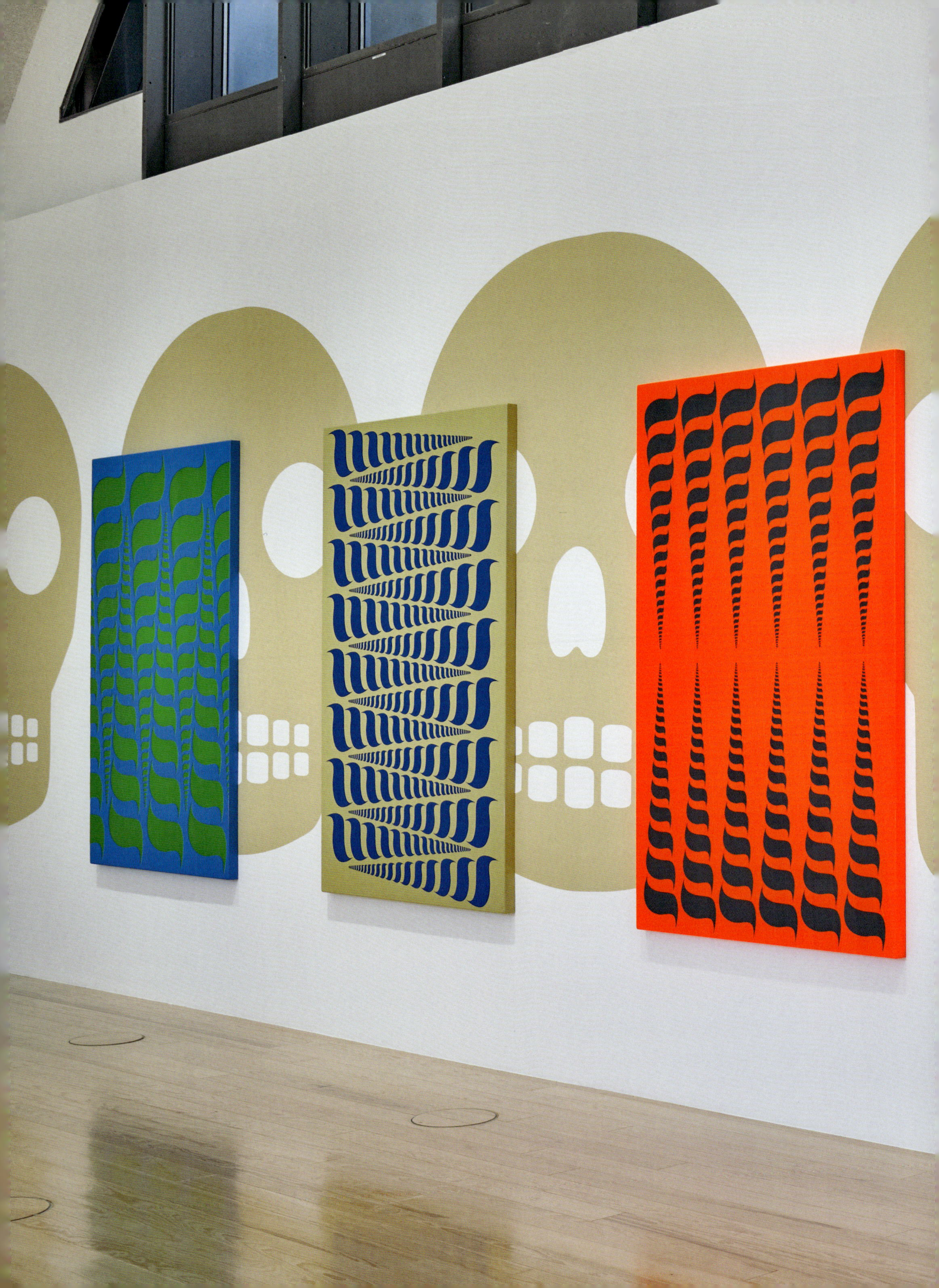

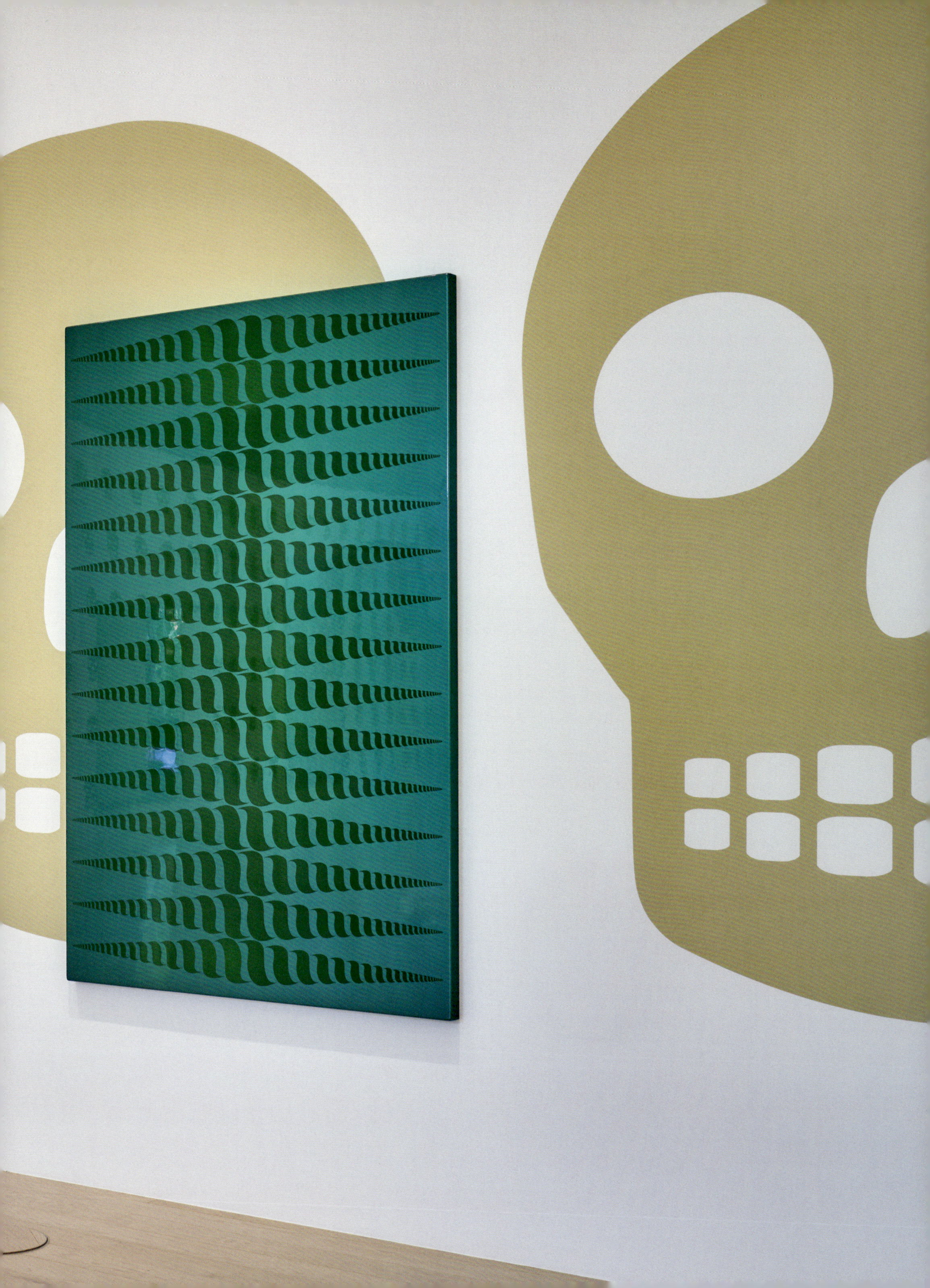

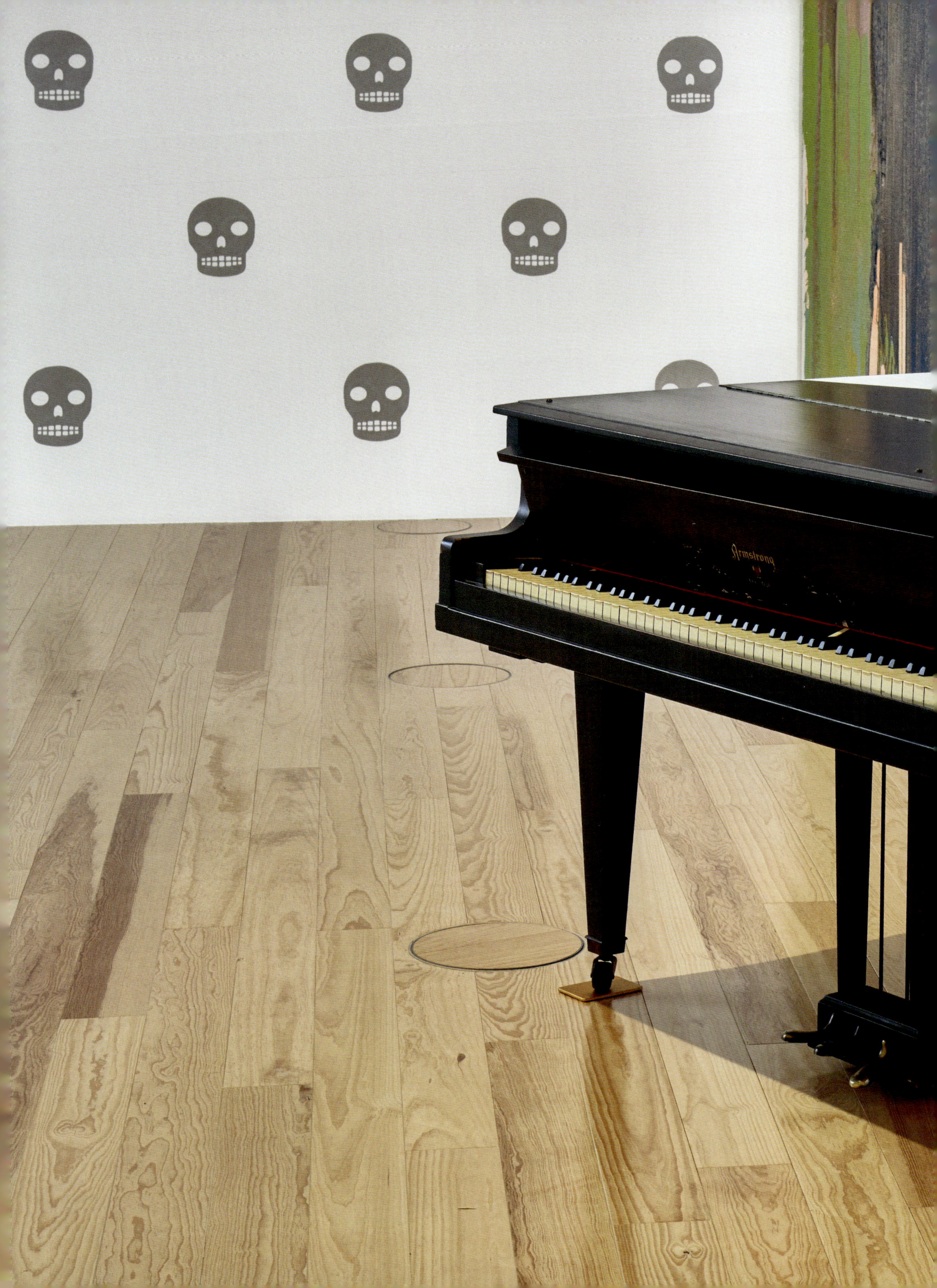
Armstrong

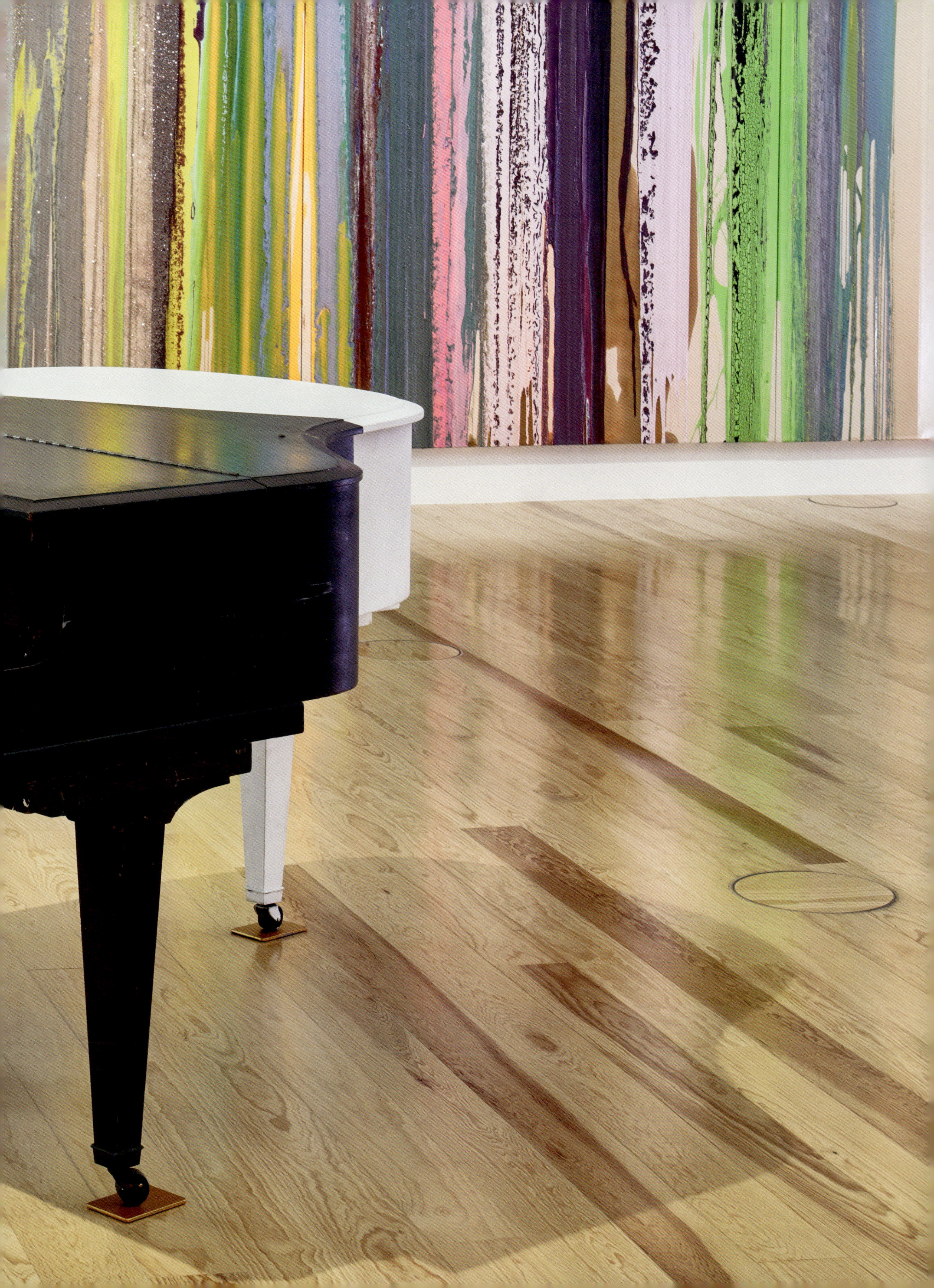

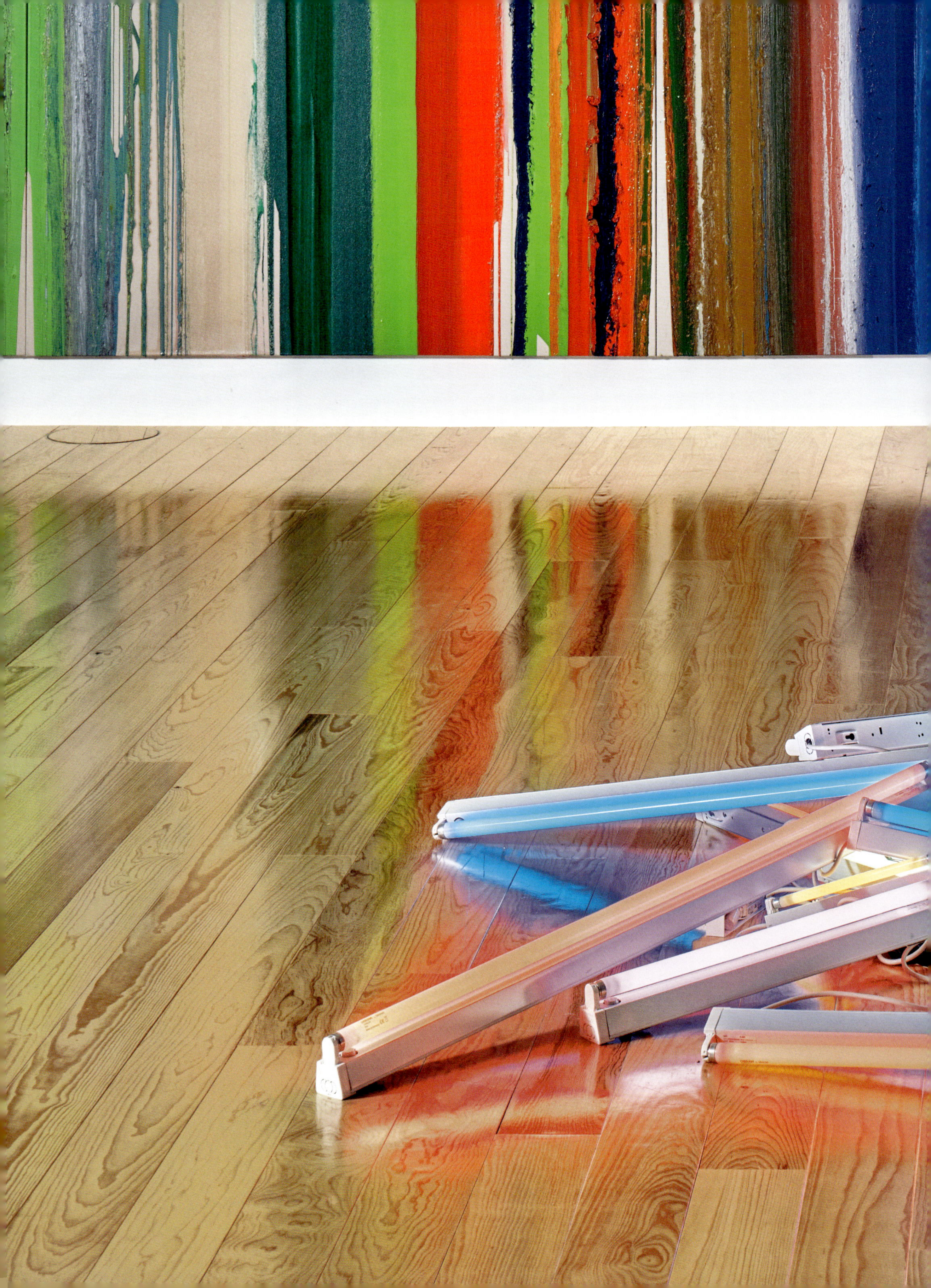

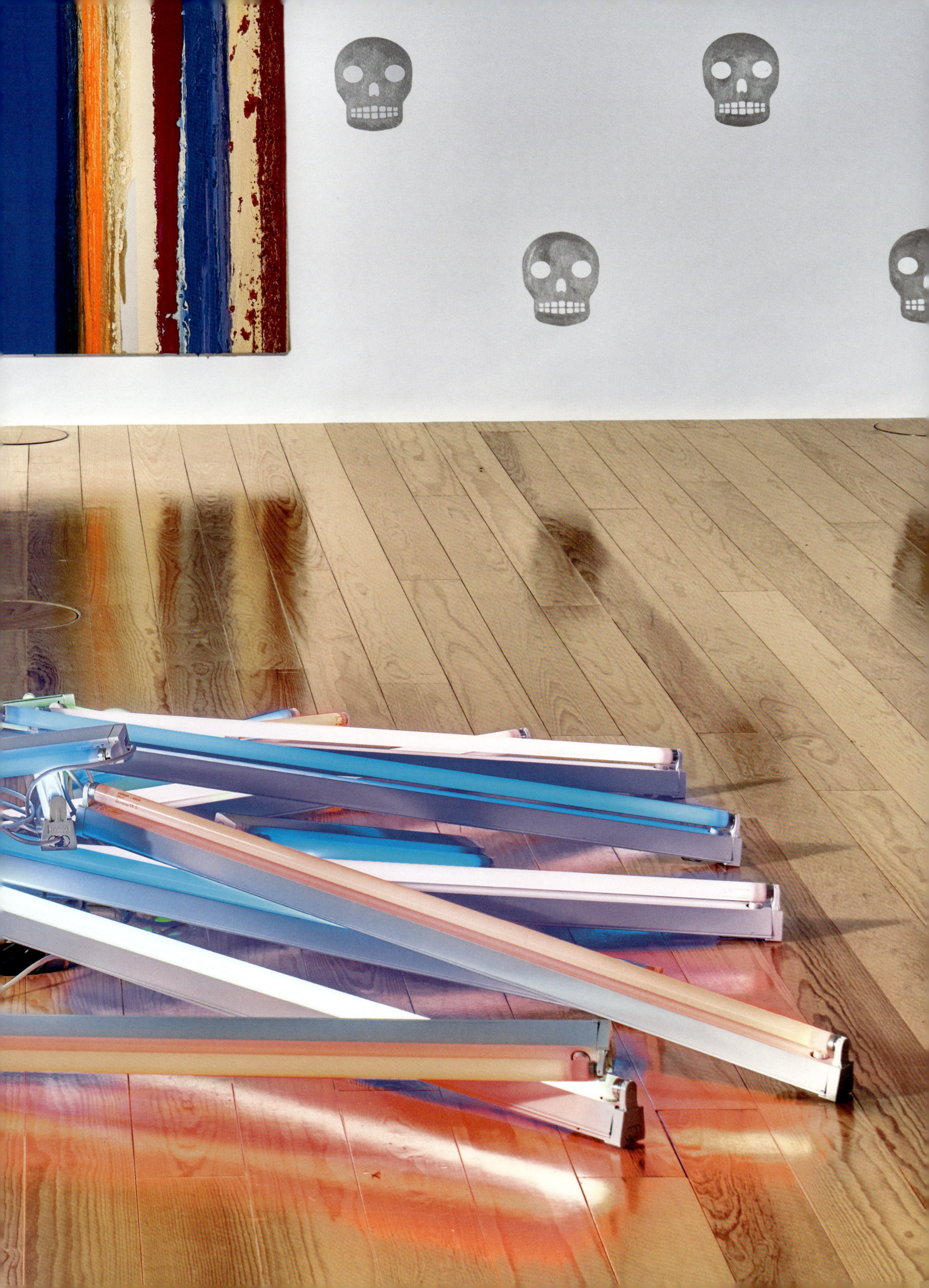

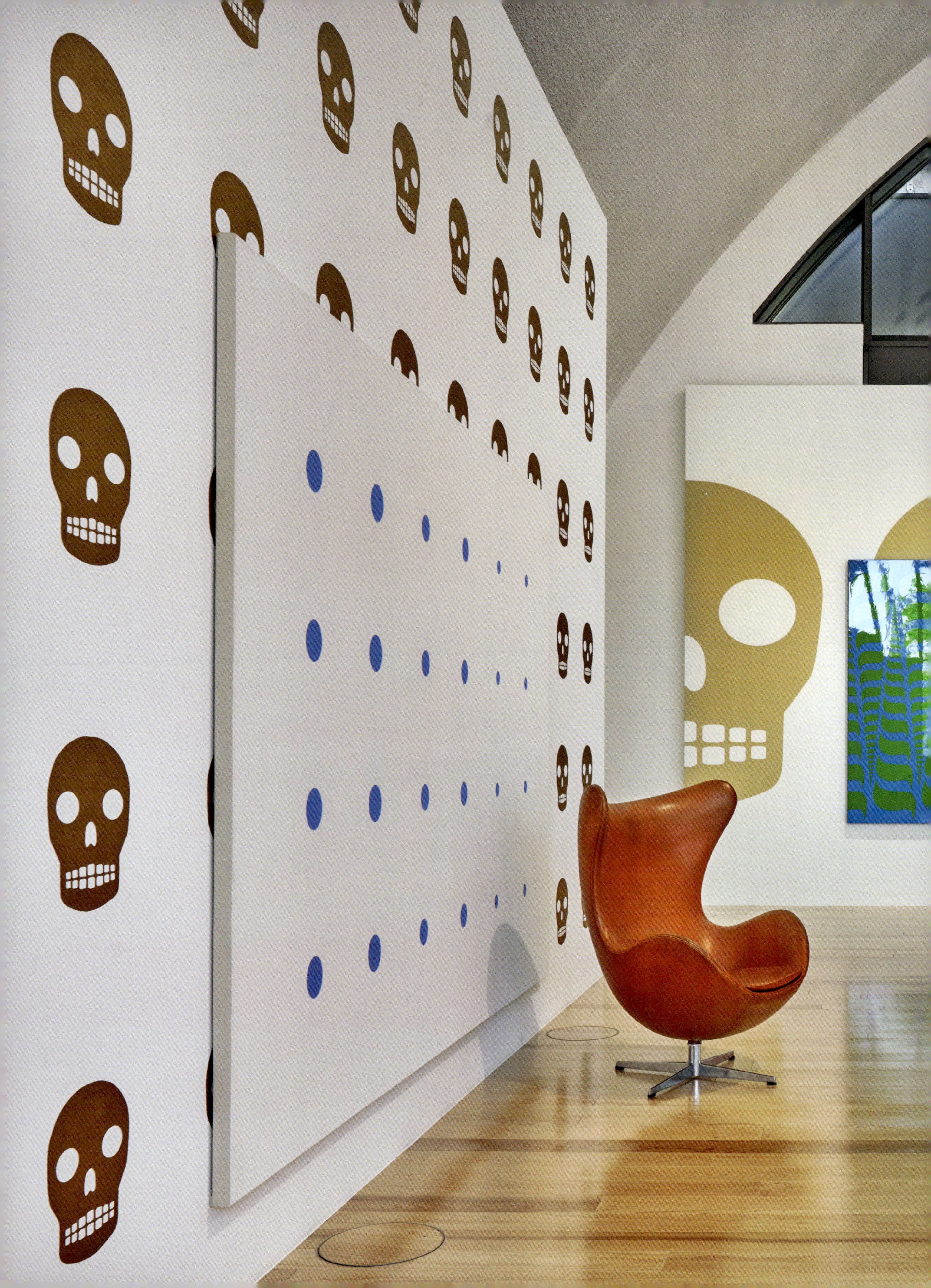

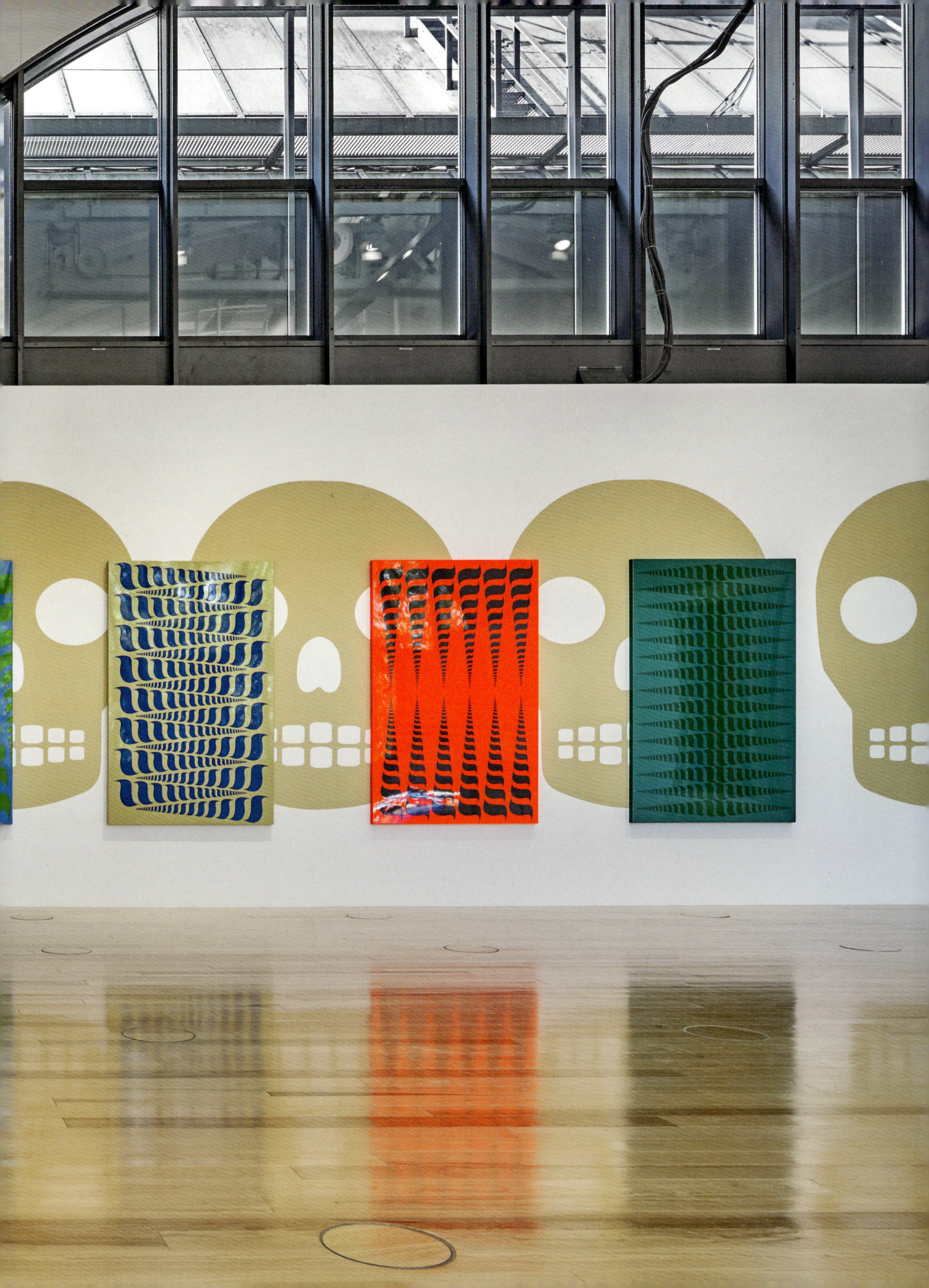

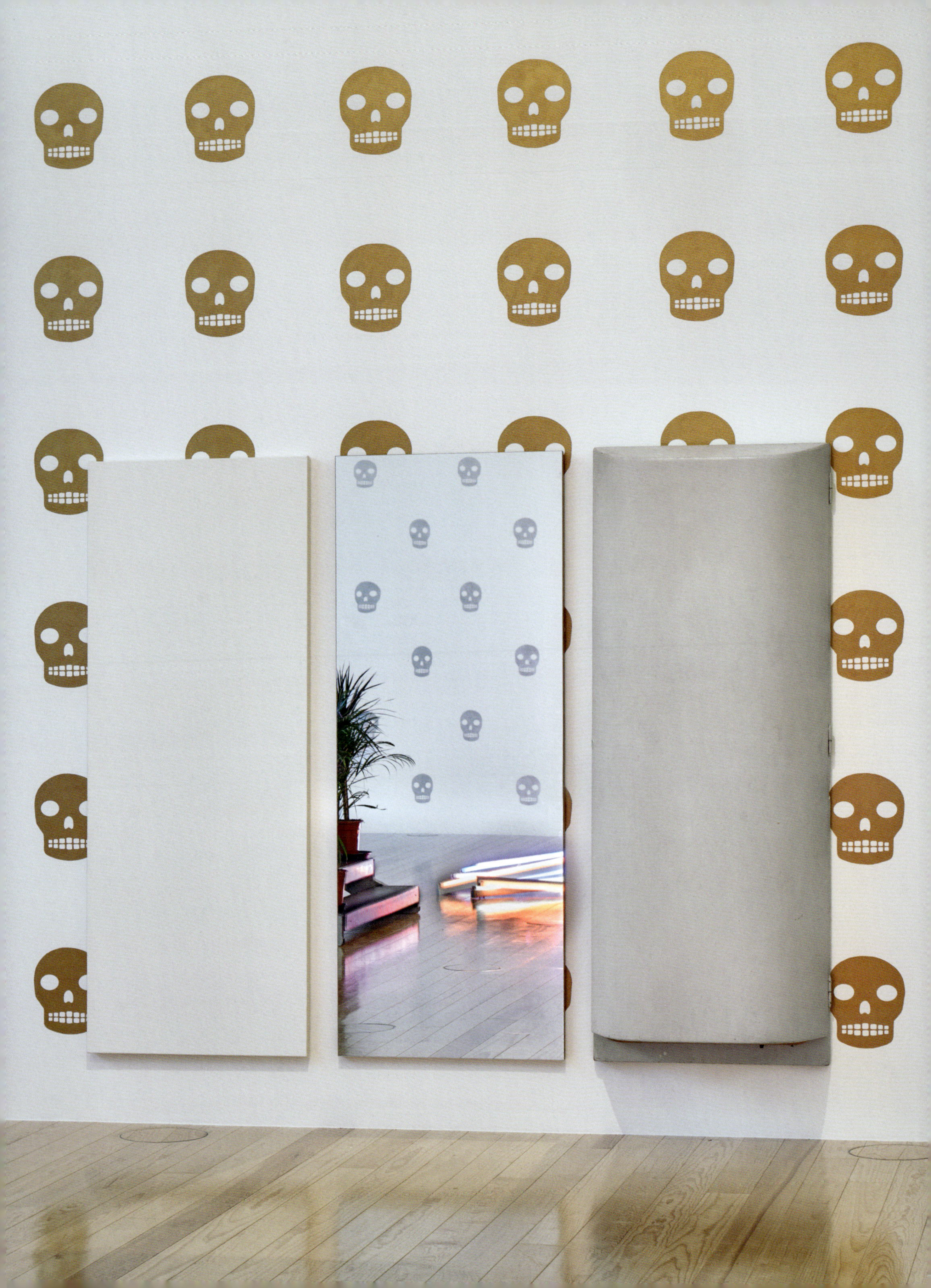

Preface

There seems to be nothing that John M Armleder cannot do. His art combines high culture and everyday life, the profound and the banal, and opens up a diverse cosmos of art-historical references. Design, Op-Art and Pop Art, Constructivism, and a close relationship to the Fluxus movement—all this is evident in Armleder's extensive oeuvre, not to mention his casual interspersing of ironic and poetic aperçus about the contemporary art world.

As one of the most important conceptual, performance, and object artists of his time, he already has a place in art history. With the installations developed for the Schirn, he has created a special exhibition experience for us: twenty disco balls turn the Schirn Rotunda into a hall of mirrors, while inside, colorful, luminous *Pour Paintings* are juxtaposed with expansive wall works and sculptures.

Armleder's playful approach to coincidence, his strategy of concealment and spontaneity provide for surprise and amazement, and actively involve the viewer. The work becomes an "event," as he himself once said. The nearly 2,300 Friends of the Schirn are delighted to intensively support this journey through the art history of the twentieth and twenty-first centuries. Although Armleder's work rejects everything conventional, the art of the seventy-year old with its contemporary and art-historical references appears perfectly staged here and will inspire us Friends of the Schirn!

Christian Strenger
Schirn Freunde e.V.

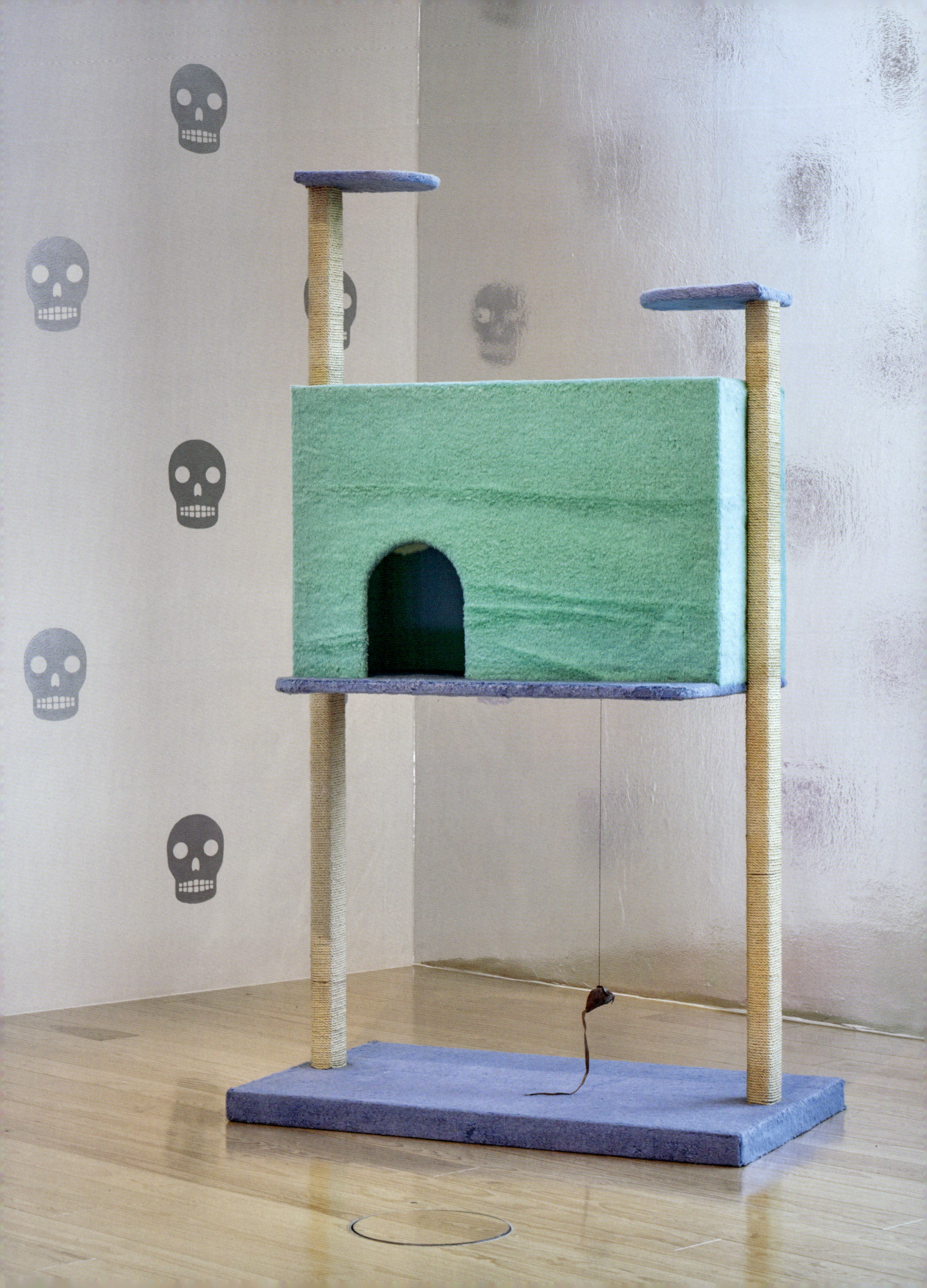

Foreword

It is an integral part of the program of the Schirn Kunsthalle Frankfurt to consistently present artists who have not been shown in Germany for a long time and whose professional peak or most prominent phase already goes back several years. In the past, their reconsideration and reexamination under changed conditions and in a changed contemporary context have often led to an interesting investigation of their current significance, as was the case, for example, with Julian Schnabel, A. R. Penck, and Peter Halley.

John M Armleder is one of the most influential contemporary artists in Europe. His unusual works are based on the formal repertoire of Modernism—Constructivism, Op-Art, Pop, gestural and abstract painting, as well as video and design. The artist imbues art-historical references from all eras with humor and makes poetic or ironic commentaries on our contemporary reality and the status of art. Armleder intertwines high culture and the mundane, coincidence and planning, profundity and triviality with a wide range of media and combines these to create an ambivalent and unique experience.

John M Armleder's work has already been shown twice at the Schirn in group exhibitions, but that was quite some time ago: in 1986 in the *Prospect* series and in 1998 in *Freie Sicht aufs Mittelmeer,* a cooperation with the Kunsthaus Zürich. Armleder's last solo exhibition in Germany was at the Kunstverein in Hanover in 2006. On the occasion of his seventieth birthday in 2018, he was honored with two major exhibitions at the Museo Madre in Naples and the Museion in Bolzano.

For the Schirn Rotunda and the large exhibition hall inside the Schirn, John M Armleder has conceived two new installations which he summarizes under the title *CA.CA.* One of Armleder's basic principles is to actively engage with each new location and to work with the existing conditions on site. The artist, who was born in Geneva in 1948, often uses elements from earlier installations and combines a wide variety of materials and media.

I would first and foremost like to thank John M Armleder for his great support in the preparation of this exhibition and the realization of his impressive work in the Schirn. We very much appreciate his extraordinary commitment and his valuable contribution to the realization of this outstanding exhibition. We would also like to thank his assistants, Lena Guévry and Ludovic Bourilly, for their reliable cooperation.

I would particularly like to thank our curator Ingrid Pfeiffer, who conceived this ambitious project in close collaboration with the artist. Her great devotion to the comprehensive preparation of the exhibition and its complex implementation is underscored by her intensive research into John M Armleder's oeuvre and creative work, which is also reflected in her differentiated, enriching contribution in this exhibition catalog. As curatorial assistant, Rebecca Herlemann stood by her with great commitment; I would like to express my sincere gratitude for her dedication, as well as for her essay in this publication.

Karin Osbahr and Lizzie Gilbert are to thank for the attentive editing of these texts and Gérard Goodrow for his sensitive translations. I would like to express my gratitude to Edition Cantz, in particular Doris Hansmann, for the fruitful cooperation. Thanks also go to Maik Stapelberg and Daniel Fritz of stapelberg&fritz for the creative design of the publication. I am also grateful to John Russo of Studioheyhey for the harmonious, tailor-made exhibition design. I would particularly like to thank Norbert Miguletz for the great photographs of John M Armleder's work at the Schirn.

My thanks furthermore go to Mehdi Chouakri. I am extremely grateful for his valuable support in the conception of the exhibition, as well as for his advice and commitment in communicating with the artist and his studio. I would also like to thank David Kordansky Gallery LA for the cooperation and kind support.

I am also sincerely grateful to the Schirn Zeitgenossen (Schirn Contemporaries), a group of private sponsors who have repeatedly and generously supported contemporary exhibitions at the Schirn, as well as to the Swiss Arts Council Pro Helvetia, which has also made a considerable contribution to the exhibition. Furthermore, with their numerous donations, members of the Board of Trustees and the Board of Directors of the Friends of the Schirn have made a significant contribution to the realization of the accompanying publication. In particular, I would like to thank Christian Strenger, the Chairman of the Friends of the Schirn, and Managing Director, Tamara Fürstin von Clary, for their personal commitment.

I would furthermore like to extend my thanks to the City of Frankfurt, in particular—as representatives of all decision-makers—Lord Mayor Peter Feldmann and the Deputy Mayor for Cultural Affairs, Ina Hartwig, for their continued support of our work at the Schirn.

This outstanding exhibition project and accompanying publication would not have been possible without the dedication of the Schirn team. For this I would like to express my sincere gratitude to all members of the staff: first of all Esther Schlicht, Head of Exhibitions, and her assistant Anna Noll, as well as Karin Grüning, Elke Walter, and Luise Leyer, for their coordination of the transport as well as for the installation and dismantling of the exhibition. I would like to thank Christian Teltz and Oliver Taschke for their technical support, Andreas Gundermann and the hanging team, and our conservator Susanne Silbernagel. Luise Bachmann, Heike Stumpf, Hannah Ruiz, and Elena Schmidt were responsible for the creative marketing and campaign design. My thanks go to Johanna Pulz, Julia Bastian, Elisabeth Pallentin, and Isabelle Hammer for their press work. I would like to thank Antonia Lagemann, together with Anuschka Berthelius, for coordinating and supervising the publication and for editing the Schirn Magazine. I would also like to extend my thanks to Chantal Eschenfelder, as well as Simone Boscheinen, Laura Heeg, Irmi Rauber, and Olga Shmakova, for the educational program. I am very grateful to Ute Seiffert and Lena Sobczinski for the development and coordination of the events at the Schirn as well as to Julia Lange and Miriam Werner, for their support of our partners and sponsors. I am also grateful to Heike Berndt, Claudia Kroh, and Tanja Stahl, as well as to Daniela Becker for her assistance in numerous matters. Finally, I would like to thank the messengers Stefan Schell and Lukas Müller, as well as Rosaria La Tona and the cleaning team; Bettina Beyermann, together with Vilizara Antalavicheva and Josef Härig, as well as all other Schirn employees who were involved in the realization of this unique exhibition and publication.

Philipp Demandt
Director
Schirn Kunsthalle Frankfurt

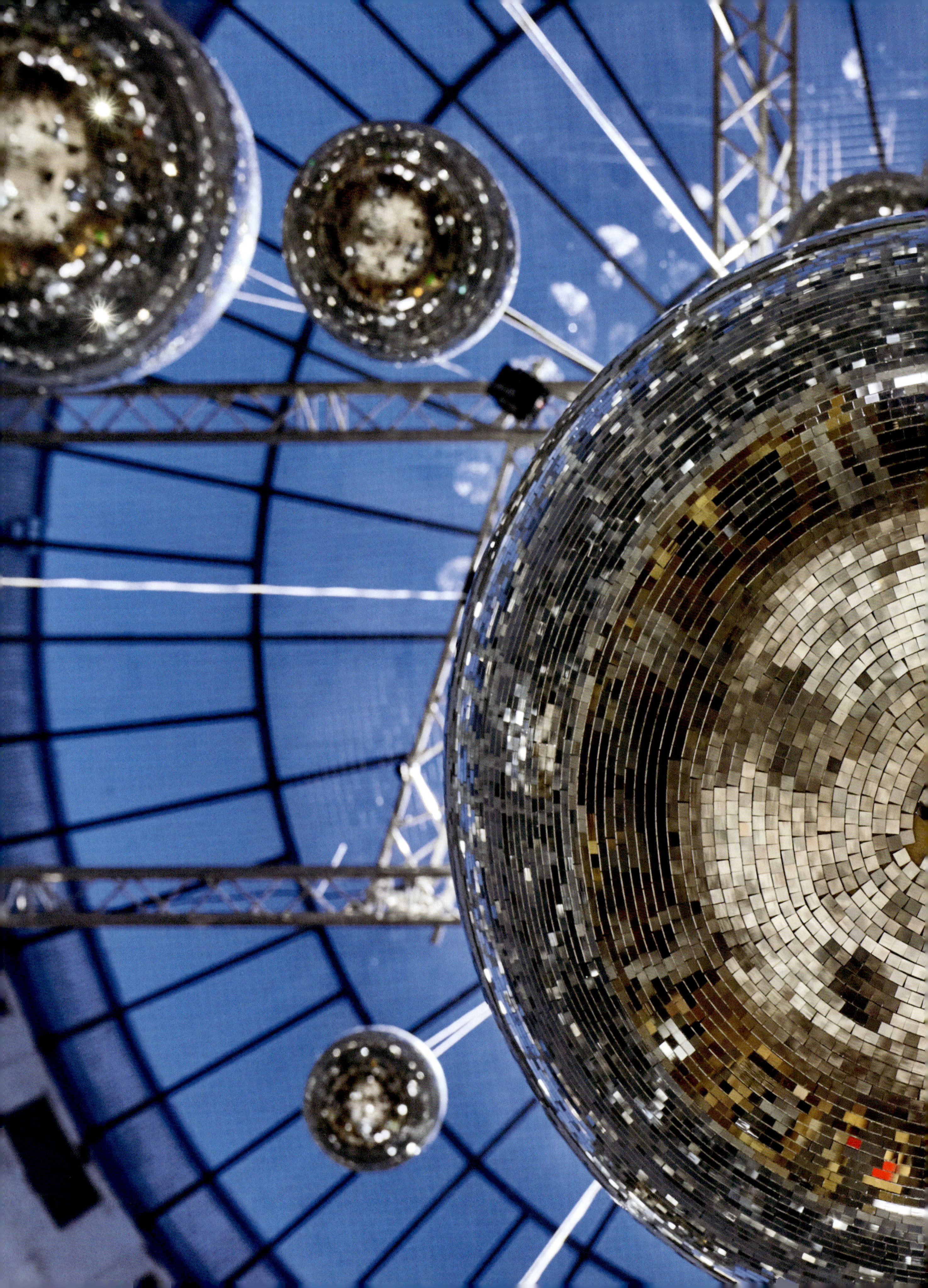

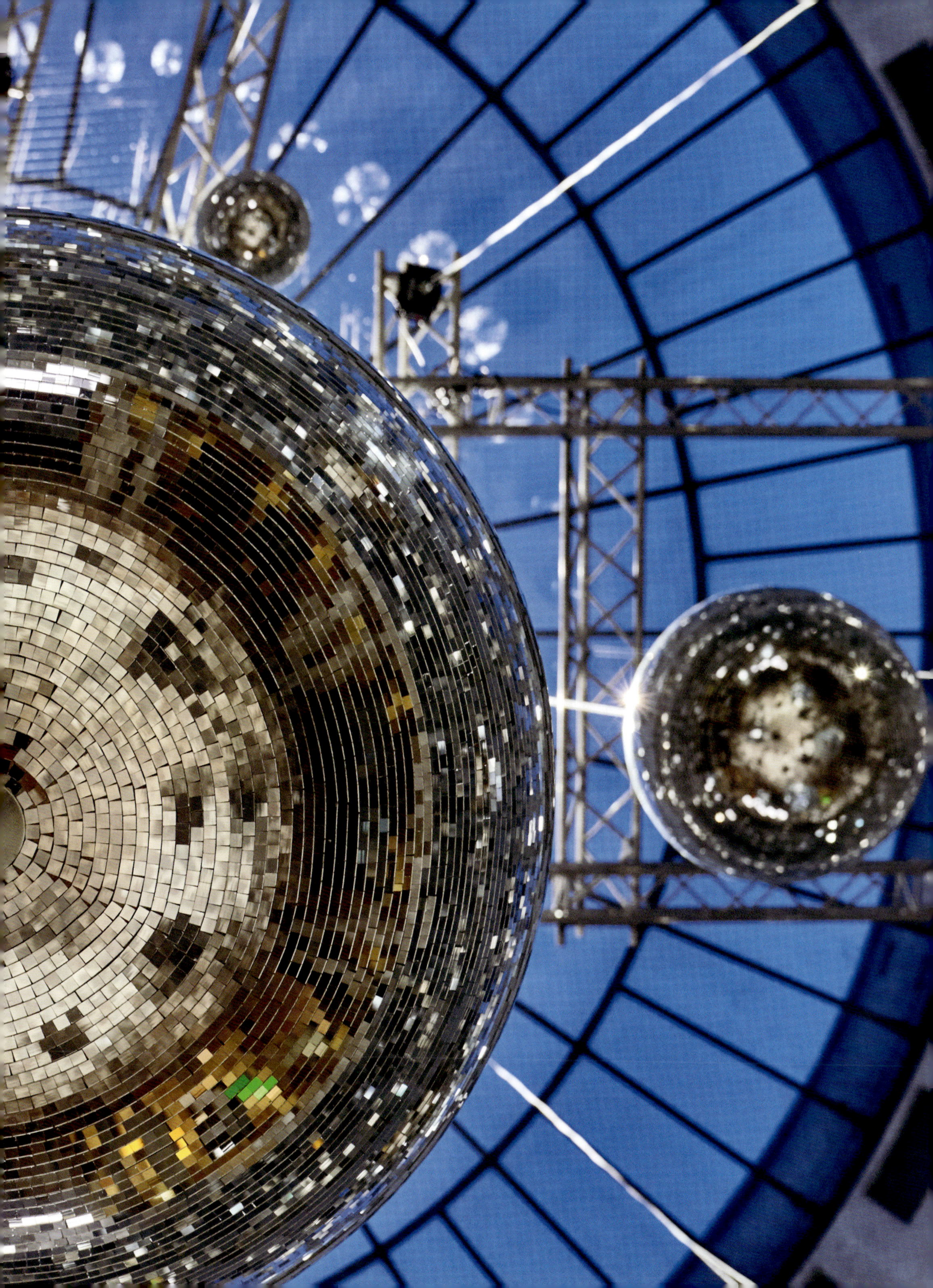

Quote—Chance—Irony
John M Armleder's Art of Open Communication

Ingrid Pfeiffer

"The joy of art remains a mystery to me, both in its production and its contemplation." John M Armleder, 1985[1]

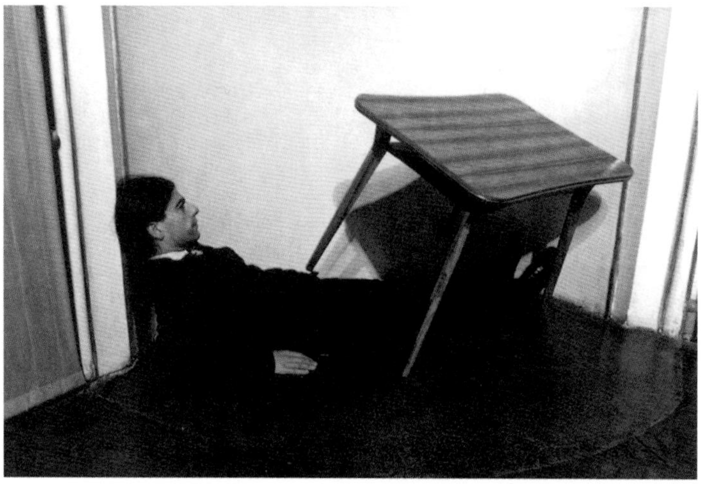

fig. 1 John M Armleder with *Furniture Sculpture* at the cultural festival *steirischer herbst '82* in Graz

1 Conversation between John M Armleder and Helmut Federle, Zurich, November 16/17, 1985, in *John M Armleder*, exh. cat. Vienna Secession, 1993, 50.

John M Armleder's art presents us as viewers with challenges that do not seem at all compatible with its casual lightness. His installations full of mirrors and colors, patterns and surfaces, disco balls and construction rods, plants, stuffed animals, old furniture, monitors, films, music, and other elements from our contemporary world leave us both fascinated and perplexed. Elegant, perfectly staged, and nimble, Armleder's work comes across as harmonious despite all its heterogeneity—at the same time, it appears hermetic and does not easily reveal itself. Is this where "banality and complexity" meet, as a critic once wrote?[2]

"My paintings are fully unreasonable," Armleder elaborates, "they escape all intelligent, discursive comprehension... What we are doing has little to do with what is thought that we're doing."[3] This statement dates back many years, but the strategy of withdrawal, evasion, and concealment can still be found in Armleder's practice today. In order to penetrate more deeply into the foundations, the prerequisites of his work, we must look at his beginnings, which form the basis for all later works.[4] What is particularly striking is that Armleder constantly quotes art history, especially the traditions of geometric abstraction and conceptual art. Colored surfaces, stripes, rings, circles, and other geometric elements in Armleder's works are familiar to us from the early years of abstraction during the era of classical modernism—a chapter of art history that has long since been closed and that seems to us today like a "heroic" time in art. Constructivism and Suprematism not only celebrated new formal inventions—e.g. abstraction—but artists also believed in the life-changing and socially transformative force in their works. Their texts were often manifestos; their struggles were heroic, whether against what they saw as outdated and anti-modern, or against massive political oppression. From Malevich to Rothko, abstract and geometric art can hardly be imagined without its spiritual dimension—for what would Malevich's *Black Square* be if one did not read into it the very big questions about space and time, about the "death" of painting, or even about the great nothingness or divinity? There is a reason why Malevich's colors are compared with the palette of Russian icon painting, and his texts also unfold on a meta-level. Although Armleder has distanced himself very far from this form of viewing art, he maintains: "I think the historical avantgardes are always in my mind, which perhaps is not the case for the young artists of today."[5] What artists have always had in common

2 Markus Brüderlin, "Ironie und Fundamentalismus. Vom Schicksal der abstrakten Kunst am Anfang der neunziger Jahre," in exh. cat. Vienna Secession 1993, 39.

3 John M Armleder in an interview with Christoph Schenker, in *Flash Art,* no. 130, October/November 1986, 68.

4 See Friederike Nymphius, *John M Armleder. Pudding Overdose* (Heidelberg: 2002), 7.

5 Helena Kontova and Giancarlo Politi, "John M Armleder. A Gentleman in the Fluxus Tradition" [interview], in *Flash Art,* no. 63, March/April 1992, 64.

is the belief that there is "progress" in art, that anyone who creates something new can be better than their predecessors, that innovation will always follow innovation. Armleder, in contrast, has long rejected this attitude. "I don't do anything different from what others have done before,"[6] has been his statement since the 1980s—it will, however, become evident that this is only possible to a limited extent, and Armleder does indeed do many things that only he can do.

When Armleder began his artistic career in the late 1960s, not only had Modernism long since passed, but Minimal Art, which was linked to the geometric tradition, was also already fading away. Pop Art had thoroughly confused the artistic value system. Even the Fluxus movement, with its search for an ephemeral art full of cheap materials and its rejection of the market value of art, was already in its late phase. Fluxus tied in with modern art by other means: here, too, the ideal goal was a closer connection between "art and life." By means of multiples, performances, and group activities, Fluxus artists rejected personal style and the individual, valuable, and expensive work of art. Ideas should always be more important than "things."

Much younger than other Fluxus artists such as John Cage, Alan Kaprow, Emmett Williams, Dick Higgins, and Ben Vautier, Armleder had his first exhibition in 1973, together with the Groupe Ecart in Geneva, which had already been founded in 1969 and for which he had written a manifesto. "Ecart" is French for "divergency"—a rejection of the concrete and definable. At this time, Armleder's parameters were already defined, at least in this respect. It was also common practice in the Groupe Ecart to revisit and recycle one's own ideas or those of others,[7] and it has continued to be so for Armleder to this day.

One of his first installations was dedicated to John Cage (fig. 2)—an acoustic conglomeration of ten audio pieces by living and deceased artists, including Fluxus artists George Brecht and Dick Higgins, as well as the "grandfathers" of Dada, such as Tristan Tzara, Kurt Schwitters, and above all Marcel Duchamp. The selection of artists refers to Armleder's personal preferences and points of reference.[8] To this day, the playful, the open, the inclusion of chance, the subversive, and the unplanned continue to be important elements in Armleder's understanding of art. The artist not only shares John Cage's interest in music, but also in Zen Buddhism, in which a certain passivity is desired, and which also allows space for the indeterminate and coincidental.[9]

6 "Suzanne Pagé im Gespräch mit John Armleder," in *John M Armleder,* exh. cat. Kunstmuseum Winterthur, 1987, 63.
7 See Nymphius 2002 (see note 4), 16.
8 See ibid., 19.
9 See ibid., 24.

Those who know Armleder are not surprised by such preferences, because letting go, being relaxed, letting things happen, even if the result is ultimately a completely different one than planned, or even if it only develops in the process—this is precisely what characterizes his working method.

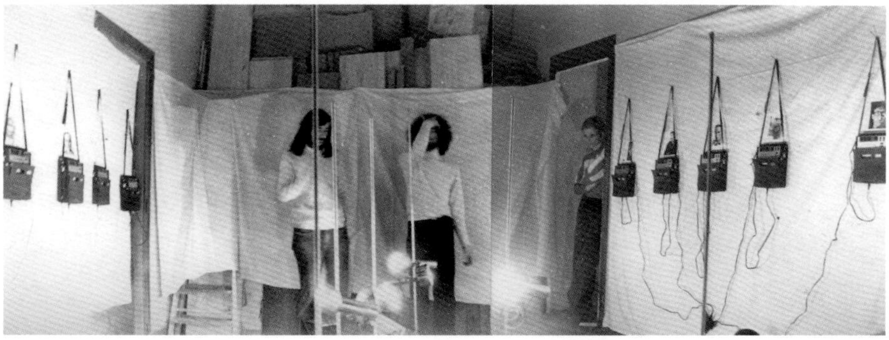

fig. 2 John M Armleder
Conversation, Etude pour John Cage sur dix bandes magnétiques, 1973

Following the Fluxus experiments of the 1970s, Armleder's formal vocabulary changed and then became almost contrary to Fluxus, especially since the 1990s: instead of "poor" materials, colorful, luminous, reflective, and seemingly glamorous surfaces dominate to this day, so that this combination with the above-mentioned Zen philosophy has even been described as "Disco Zen."[10] Nevertheless, to this day, Armleder's performances are still based on the basic principles of the Fluxus artists: "[...] we also performed the scripts of the Fluxus people for many years and I still do that, as a matter of fact."[11]

Armleder's best-known works include the *Furniture Sculptures,* geometric painting combined with found and used everyday furniture and musical instruments (fig. 3), which he produced from 1979 onwards. These works reflect Armleder's concept of combinatorics, not only of media (painting) and objects (furniture), but also in the superimposition of signs and the mixing of contexts, since the viewer now has a part to play in the interpretation. Here, for the first time, there is a mix of high and low, of familiar forms of art history and design, as well as mundane objects of daily use. To this day, Armleder does not avoid such comparisons and references but incorporates them, aware of the fact that trivial culture enables a different form of communication with the viewer. There are recognition effects but, at the same time, these are ironically broken and ambivalently alienated. Armleder

10 Alessandro Rabottini, "Disco Zen" [interview], in exh. cat. *John Armleder. Voltes IV. Special Guest 2,* exh. cat. Galleria d'Arte Moderna e Contemporanea di Bergamo (Milan: 2004).

11 Henri Neuendorf, "John Armleder on Why Art Is more Important than Artists" [interview], in *artnet.news,* January 19, 2017, URL: https://news.artnet.com/art-world/john-armleder-interview-822530 (last accessed on May 18, 2019).

attracts the viewer to familiar terrain, so to speak, but the familiar turns out to be merely ostensible, and all insight is blurred—the artist always maintains an ironic distance. "My work has a certain degree of distance, which I enjoy very much," Armleder explains.[12]

Historically speaking, with their return to geometry, the artists in Europe and the USA also reacted to the new "wild," figurative painting of the 1980s. Through his time in New York, Armleder was in contact with American neo-geo artists such as Peter Halley, Haim Steinbach, and Jeff Koons, who combined elements of Minimalism with those of Pop Art but, as a European, he was more strongly influenced by the tradition of the European avant-garde.

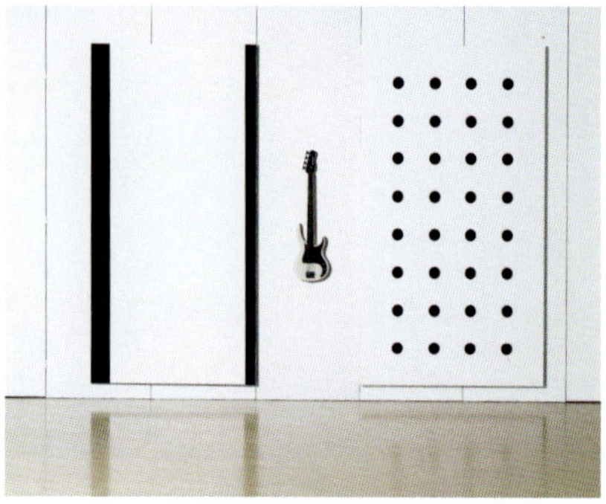

fig. 3 John M Armleder
Furniture Sculpture 132, For the love of Daisy, 1986

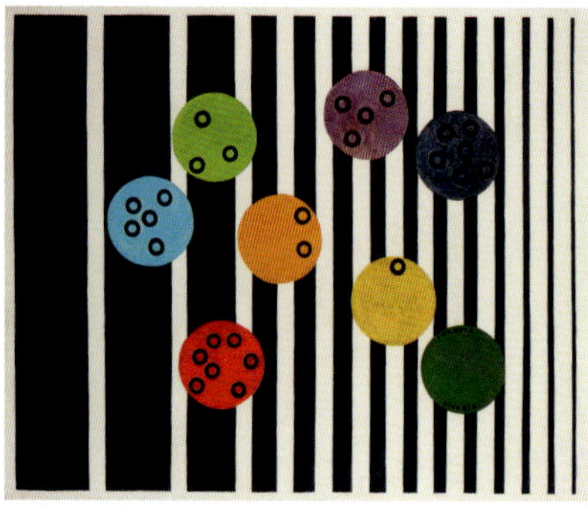

fig. 4 Francis Picabia
Volucelle [II], 1923

While the *Furniture Sculptures* still tied in with classical image formats, that is to say they had a spatial boundary and only expanded, so to speak, forward into the space, Armleder extended the forms and patterns to such an extent that the entire wall, the entire exhibition space was included: "In a way, I'm a believer in total confusion between surface and content."[13] Armleder points out that he began using this "all-over" process because he and other artists wanted to liberate themselves from the compulsion to compose. The frequently used dots and stripes, regularly or randomly distributed on the wall, find their precursors in the work of Francis Picabia, an artist whose numerous changes of style and playful irony were a model for Armleder's own approach (fig. 4). "I am like a Picabia kind of person, who did one different thing after another and never stopped doing different things," Armleder describes his working process.[14]

12 Kontova / Politi 1992 (see note 5), 68.
13 Rabottini 2004 (see note 10), 38.
14 Neuendorf 2017 (see note 11).

The randomness of the result is the main feature of Armleder's large-format *Pour Paintings* (ill. pp. 30/31), in which every principle of composition dissolves. Different materials—cheap, expensive, and in some cases incompatible—are mixed, poured together, and produce a result that remains as it is. The artist accepts it as part of the process: "I am a chance freak: paradise gained through randomness," Armleder explains. "The Great Random obliterates any totalitarian policy. It's an immense equalizer paired with an enhancer."[15]

As a precursor to these *Pour Paintings,* Armleder cites the largely unknown American painter Larry Poons (fig. 5), who in the 1970s referred in turn to works by Morris Louis (fig. 6) from the early 1960s. Such a constant "recycling" of forms—also described as "refocusing"[16]—plays a key role in Armleder's concept, for he constantly questions the role of contemporary art in an irretrievably transformed and permanently changing cultural system. Like many other artists in the 1980s, Armleder felt he had to confront the ubiquitous "states of exhaustion of modernity"[17] with new strategies.

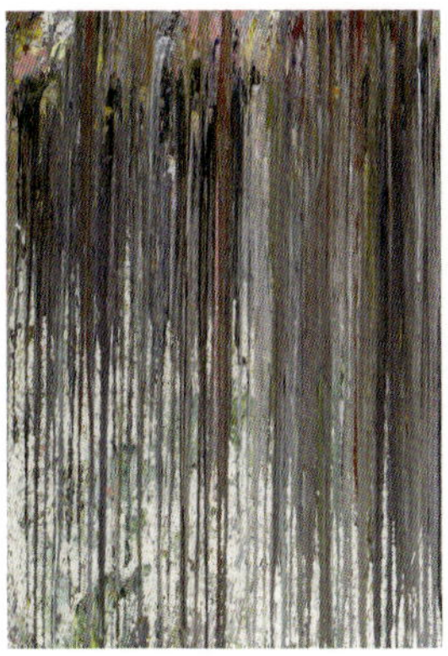

fig. 5 Larry Poons
Untitled (18-A),
1976

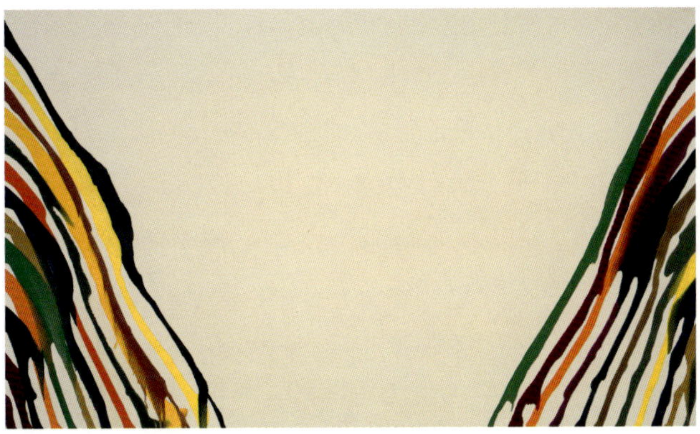

fig. 6 Morris Louis
Beta Zeta, 1960/61

There is a reason why Armleder likes to use mirrors and acrylic glass, disco balls and fluorescent tubes in his installations. What we see is ourselves or a will-o'-the-wisp of reality, broken by reflective surfaces, because, according to Armleder, "reality" as such does not exist. The artist perceives many things as relative—without really being cynical about this. In an interview with his artist friend Helmut Federle, Armleder describes his own eclecticism of forms and means and his "silent disclosure of all these contradictions."[18]

15 Conversation between John M Armleder and Raphaela Platow [October 2006], in *John M Armleder. Too Much Is Not Enough,* exh. cat. Kunstverein Hannover (Heidelberg: 2006), 103.
16 Nymphius 2002 (see note 4), 30.
17 Markus Brüderlin, "Das geflügelte Bild oder Malerei als Wiederholung. Iterativismus in der Abstraktion," in *Kunstforum International,* no. 105, January/February 1990, 110–2.
18 Armleder / Federle 1993 (see note 1), 49.

Armleder combines and confronts many heterogeneous things—geometric forms versus poured paintings, *objets trouvés* in the tradition of Marcel Duchamp with elements from the worlds of fashion, music, and everyday life. "To a certain degree I mixed everything together," Armleder states.[19] He influenced trends—and, to this day, many young artists still refer to him as a role model. In contrast to his younger successors, however, Armleder still knows the origin and meaning of what he quotes and is therefore far from an understanding of art for which art history is merely a quarry from which to indiscriminately extract that which is necessary. Although Armleder reflects this development of "anything goes," which began in the 1980s and continues to this day, even when he does (or tries to do) this in an ostensibly value-free manner, he is indeed part of a generation that still felt the painful loss of utopia. A certain melancholy always flashes through when Armleder talks about the art of the past, which he quotes, recasts, and transforms into something different, something permanently new. "Using the same pen doesn't mean writing the same text," Armleder argues. "Even if it's the same words, as a matter of fact, or the same paper. It's another day, it's another planet [...]."[20]

The artist believes that the most important element lies in the triangular relationship between the work, the space, and the viewer—it is only in this combination that the specific meaning develops, which is why many installations are created on site. "I don't define my work. It always performs differently, for each single onlooker, and so connects to various levels of perception. I still like the idea of referring to work as events."[21]

The "event" that Armleder has realized in the Schirn is called *CA.CA.* and consists of two rooms that are very different but which together contain many of Armleder's themes: in the Rotunda, the entrance area of the Schirn, the artist has hung twenty slowly rotating disco balls of various sizes on several different levels, which are reflected in the windows that have been covered with mirrored foil. The work is visually overwhelming and adapts itself perfectly to the given spatial conditions. In its mixture of luster and cheap decoration, it contains that playful element which is characteristic of Armleder's concept. In the large exhibition hall inside the Schirn, which contains a new installation, Armleder presents his well-known *Pour Paintings,* as well as wall pieces specially adapted to the site. As always, he spontaneously oriented himself to the local conditions shortly before the start of the exhibition and with the

19 Kontova / Politi 1992 (see note 5), 64.

20 Spark Vett, Parker Williams, and Sylvie Fleury, "John Armleder: At Any Speed" [conversation], in *Parkett,* no. 50/51, 1997, 42–7, here 47.

21 Rabottini 2004 (see note 10), 38.

participation of everyone involved. Over 400 stylized skulls in silver, gold, and ivory—a motif that he has often used for mural paintings in the style of wallpaper—cover the walls in various sizes. Armleder has never before used this vanitas motif, which can be found in the oeuvres of most great modern artists, from Pablo Picasso to Andy Warhol, in such a consistent and space-filling manner. Yet again, banality and complexity meet and result in the often overlapping mix of context and meaning which is so characteristic of Armleder's work. Among the sculptures that are mounted on the wall and can be counted as part of the earlier *Furniture Sculptures* is an upside-down, double children's slide—a symbol of our present, which is marked by infantile megalomania. Armleder himself always avoids such interpretations but is extremely tolerant when we as viewers develop them.

Armleder's art is a challenge, a conceptual tour de force through the art history of the twentieth and twenty-first centuries with its developments and intellectual consequences. It is particularly contemporary because it conceals its sources but does not deny them. It is unique, although and precisely because the artist rejects conventional innovations. It is a nimble, seductive form of conceptual art that not only satisfies the eye and the senses, but also—if one allows it—the critical mind.

Biography John M Armleder

Rebecca Herlemann

1948 John Michael Armleder is born in Geneva on June 24, 1948.

since 1963 Musical and other activities with the Groupe Luc Bois and the Groupe Max Bolli, Geneva

1966/67 Studies at the Ecole des beaux-arts in Geneva (one semester in the painting department and one semester in various studios)

1969 Participation in the mixed media course *The Black Box* with John Epstein at the Glamorgan Summer School, Wales
Foundation of the Groupe Ecart with Patrick Lucchini and Claude Rychner. "Ecart" is French for "divergency"—it refers here to the group's rejection of the concrete and definable. The group organizes exhibitions, performances, concerts, and conferences

1972 Armleder founds Ecart Publications, which publishes works by members of the Groupe Ecart as well as by Peter Downsbrough, Robert Filliou, Dan Graham, Genesis P-Orridge, Sarkis, Endre Tót, Lawrence Weiner, and others

1973 Foundation of Galerie Ecart, Rue Plantamour 6, Geneva (as of 1979, together with the Centre d'art contemporain at Rue d'Italie 16). Exhibitions with members of the Groupe Ecart, as well as with Joseph Beuys, John Cage, Giuseppe Chiari, Braco Dimitrijević, Dick Higgins, George Maciunas, Olivier Mosset, Daniel Spoerri, Ben Vautier, Jan Voss, Andy Warhol, and others

1974 Foundation of the Ecart Performance Groupe

1975 Opening of the bookstore Ecart / Books as part of the gallery; as of 1980, together with Fluxkiosk

1976 Co-founder of the International Institutions Register (I.I.R.), the aim of which is to compile a list of "artistically initiated counter-institutions"

1977 Foundation of Leathern Wing Scribble Press; co-founder of the artists' cooperative Laboratorio, Milan; founding member and Representative Director for Europe of Associated Art Publishers (the nomadic seat of the association is located in the USA)

1977–79 Swiss Federal Art Scholarship

1979 The first *Furniture Sculptures* are created—geometric painting combined with found and used everyday furniture and musical instruments.

since 1980 Participation of Ecart at the Art Basel with its own stand, where various artists are presented on a daily basis since 1981 Armleder organizes exhibitions by Alison Knowles, Peter Suter, and Ben Vautier in his studio in the Halles de l'Ile.

1984 First solo exhibition at the John Gibson Gallery, New York. Numerous other exhibitions follow.
Organization of the exhibition *Peinture abstraite,* Ecart, Geneva, with works by members of the group as well as by Helmut Federle, Lucio Fontana, Sol LeWitt, Verena Loewensberg, Robert Mangold, Gerhard Merz, Olivier Mosset, Robert Motherwell, Blinky Palermo, Gerwald Rockenschaub, Robert Ryman, Jean-Frédéric Schnyder, and Otto Zitko

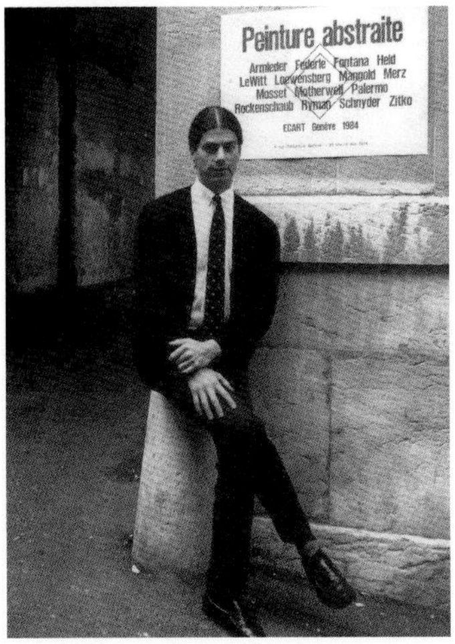

John M Armleder
Exhibition *Peinture abstraite,* Geneva 1984

1986 John M Armleder represents Switzerland at the 42nd Biennale di Venezia.

since 1987 Edition of multiples by Olivier Mosset and other artists
Large solo exhibition at the Kunstmuseum Winterthur / L'Arc Musée d'Art Moderne de la Ville de Paris / Kunstverein für die Rheinlande und Westfalen, Düsseldorf / Neue Nationalgalerie, Berlin
Participation in *Documenta 8,* Museum Fridericianum and Orangerie, Kassel

since 1989 Second studio in New York, with frequent stays there

1992–2000 Member of the Swiss Federal Commission for the Visual Arts, Bern

1993 Solo exhibition at the Vienna Secession

1995–2013 Professor at the Braunschweig University of Art (HBK) and the Ecole cantonale d'art de Lausanne (ECAL)

1997 Group exhibition *Ecart 1967–1982* at the Musée d'art moderne et contemporain, Geneva

1999 Solo exhibition *at any speed* at the Kunsthalle Baden-Baden

2018 On the occasion of Armleder's seventieth birthday, retrospectives take place at the Museion, Bolzano, and the Madre museum, Naples.

Bibliografie / Bibliography

2019 *Ecart. Genève 1969–1982,* hrsg. von / ed. by Lionel Bovier und / and Christophe Chérix, Ausst.-Kat. / exh. cat. MAMCO Genf, Köln / Cologne.

2016 Françoise Jaunin, *John Armleder. Du minimalisme à la saturation,* Lausanne.
Eye attack. Op art og kinetisk kunst, 1950–1970, hrsg. von / ed. by Tine Colstrup u.a., Ausst.-Kat. / exh. cat. Louisiana Museum of Modern Art, Humlebæk.
Split – Spiegel, Licht, Reflexion, hrsg. von / ed. by Christiane Schaufler-Münch u.a., Ausst.-Kat. / exh. cat. Schauwerk Sindelfingen, Bielefeld.

2015 *John Armleder. Out! (Out!),* hrsg. von / ed. by Lionel Bovier, Zürich.

2013 *Ecart (1969–1980),* hrsg. von / ed. by Lionel Bovier, Ausst.-Kat. / exh. cat. Charles H. Scott Gallery, Emily Carr Institute of Art & Design Vancouver, Zürich.
John Armleder – Overload, hrsg. von / ed. by Galerie Andrea Caratsch, Ausst.-Kat. / exh. cat. Galerie Andrea Caratsch, Zürich.

2012 *John M Armleder – Selected Furniture Sculptures 1979–2012,* hrsg. von / ed. by Gianni Jetzer, Ausst.-Kat. / exh. cat. Swiss Institute – Contemporary Art, New York.

2011 *Away,* hrsg. von / ed. by Gregory Volk u.a. / et al., Ausst.-Kat. / exh. cat. Peggy Guggenheim Collection, Venedig / Venice.

2006 *John Armleder – about nothing. Works on paper 1962–2007,* Ausst.-Kat. / exh. cat. Institute of Contemporary Art, University of Pennsylvania, Philadelphia, Philadelphia.
John M Armleder. Too much is not enough, hrsg. von / ed. by Stephan Berg, Ausst.-Kat. / exh. cat. Kunstverein Hannover und / and Rose Art Museum of Brandeis University, Waltham, Heidelberg.
John M Armleder: amor vacui, horror vacui, Ausst.-Kat. / exh. cat. Mamco – Musée d'art moderne et contemporain, Genf / Geneva.

2005 *John Armleder: PFCBCDRRSRGBMNF PCLSPSBMPFCBS,* hrsg. von / ed. by BSI art collection Lugano, Zürich.
Before the End. John Armleder, Ausst.-Kat. / exh. cat. Le Consortium, Centre d'Art Contemporain, Dijon.
About nothing. Arbeiten auf Papier 1964–2004, hrsg. von / ed. by Beatrix Ruf, Ausst.-Kat. / exh. cat. Kunsthalle Zürich, Zürich.
Lionel Bovier (Hrsg. / ed.), *John Armleder,* Paris und / and New York.
Flashback: eine Revision der Kunst der 80er Jahre, hrsg. von / ed. by Philipp Kaiser, Ausst.-Kat. / exh. cat. Museum für Gegenwartskunst Basel, Ostfildern-Ruit.

2004 *John Armleder: Yellow Pages,* hrsg. von / ed. by Team 404, Ausst.-Kat. / exh. cat. Mamco – Musée d'art moderne et contemporain, Genf / Geneva, Genf / Geneva und / and Zürich.
John Armleder u.a., *Indigenous Wine in Friuli Venezia Giulia,* Mailand / Milan.
L'Œuvre multiplié, catalogue raisonné des estampes et multiples édités à fin 2003, hrsg. von / ed. by Christoph Chérix und / and Rainer Michael Mason, Genf / Geneva.
Special Guest. John Armleder – Voltes IV, hrsg. von / ed. by Giacinto di Pietrantonio und / and Alessandro Rabottini, Ausst.-Kat. / exh. cat. Galleria d'Arte Moderna e Contemporanea Bergamo, Mailand / Milan.

2003 John Armleder, *Recipes Friuli Venezia Giulia,* Mailand / Milan.

2002 Frederike Nymphius, *John M Armleder. Pudding Overdose,* Heidelberg.
Wallpaintings & Wallpieces, catalogue raisonné des peintures murales et autres pieces murales, hrsg. von / ed. by Lionel Bovier, Le Magasin, Grenoble.
Parker Williams, *Collected Interviews with John M Armleder,* Dijon und / and Genf / Geneva.

2001 *Art > Music: Rock, Pop, Techno,* hrsg. von / ed. by Sue Cramer, Ausst.-Kat. / exh. cat. Museum of Contemporary Art Sydney, Sydney.

2000 *Projects 72: John Armleder, Pjotr Uklanski,* hrsg. von / ed. by Lilian Tone und / and Anne Umland, Ausst.-Kat. / exh. cat. MoMA, New York.

1999 *John M. Armleder: at any speed,* hrsg. von / ed. by Margrit Brehm, Ausst.-Kat. / exh. cat. Staatliche Kunsthalle Baden-Baden und / and Holderbank Aargau, Ostfildern.

1997 *John Armleder,* hrsg. von / ed. by Anna Dauer u.a. / et al., Ausst.-Kat. / exh. cat. Fondazione Antonio Ratti, Mailand / Milan.
Lionel Bovier und / and Christophe Chérix (Hrsg.), *L'Irrésolution commune d'un engagement* équivoque, *Ecart 1969–1982,* Genf / Geneva.
Home Sweet Home, Ausst.-Kat. / exh. cat. Deichtorhallen Hamburg, Hamburg.

1995 *Pittura Immedia,* Ausst.-Kat. / exh. cat. Neue Galerie im Landesmuseum Joanneum und / and Künstlerhaus Graz, Klagenfurt.

1994 *John M Armleder,* Ausst.-Kat. / exh. cat. Le Capitou Centre d'art contemporain Fréjus, Mailand / Milan.
Das Jahrhundert des Multiple. Von Duchamp bis zur Gegenwart, hrsg. von / ed. by Zdenek Felix, Ausst.-Kat. / exh. cat. Deichtorhallen Hamburg, Stuttgart.

1993 *Playtime, une exposition de peinture,* Ausst.-Kat. / exh. cat. Le Capitou Centre d'art contemporain, Fréjus.
John M Armleder: to choose, Arbeiten 1969–1992, hrsg. von / ed. by Wiener Secession, Ausst.-Kat. / exh. cat. Wiener Secession, Wien / Vienna.
Post Human, hrsg. von / ed. by Jeffrey Deitch, Ausst.-Kat. / exh. cat. Deichtorhallen, Hamburg.

1992 *Miniatuur – Museum,* Ausst.-Kat. / exh. cat. Reflex Modern Art Gallery Amsterdam.
John M Armleder, Pour Paintings 1982–1992, hrsg. von / ed. by Marja Bosma, Ausst.-Kat. / exh. cat. Centraal Museum, Utrecht.

1991 *John M Armleder,* Ausst.-Kat. / exh. cat. Galleria Paolo Vitolo, Rom / Rome.
Extra Muros, Zeitgenössische Schweizer Kunst, hrsg. von / ed. by E. Charrière u.a. / et al., Ausst.-Kat. / exh. cat. Musée des Beaux-Arts La Chaux-de-Fonds et al., Bern.

1990 *John M Armleder, Furniture Sculpture: 1980–1990,* hrsg. von / ed. by Claude Ritschard, Ausst.-Kat. / exh. cat. Musée Rath, Genf / Geneva.

1988 *Furniture as Art. Recent Tendencies in Sculpture,* hrsg. von / ed. by Karel Schampers und / and Talitha Schoon, Ausst.-Kat. / exh. cat. Museum Boymans van Beuningen, Rotterdam.
Escultura y dibujo. Cuatro artsitas de Suiza. Armleder, Disler, Müller, Stalder, hrsg. von / ed. by Martin Kunz, Ausst.-Kat. / exh. cat. Circulo de belles artes, Madrid.
Schlaf der Vernunft, hrsg. von / ed. by Veit Loers, Ausst.-Kat. / exh. cat. Museum Fridericianum, Kassel.

1987 *John M Armleder,* hrsg. von / ed. by Dieter Schwarz, Ausst.-Kat. / exh. cat. Kunstmuseum Winterthur et al., Winterthur.
John Armleder u.a., *Ecrits et entretiens,* Musée de la Peinture, Grenoble, Maison de la Culture, St. Etienne.

1986 *John M Armleder, Olivier Mosset,* hrsg. von / ed. by Veit Loers, Ausst.-Kat. / exh. cat. Städtische Galerie Regensburg et al., Regensburg.
Reconstruct/ Deconstruct, hrsg. von / ed. by Robert Nickas, Ausst.-Kat. / exh. cat. John Gibson Gallery, New York.
John Armleder. Paintings and Furniture Sculpture, Ausst.-Kat. / exh. cat. Lisson Gallery, London.
Origins, Originality + Beyond. The Italian Supplement, The 6th Biennale of Sydney, Sydney.
John M Armleder. Biennale de Venise, hrsg. von / ed. by Office fédéral de la culture, Ausst.-Kat. / exh. cat. Biennale di Venezia, Pavillon Suisse, Bern.
Geometria Nova, hrsg. von / ed. by Zdenek Felix, Ausst.-Kat. / exh. cat. Münchener Kunstverein et al., München / Munich.

1984 *Zeichen, Fluten, Signale: neukonstruktiv und parallel,* hrsg. von / ed. by Rosemarie Schwarzwälder, Ausst.-Kat. / exh. cat. Galerie nächst St. Stephan, Wien / Vienna.

1983 *John M Armleder. Arbeiten auf Papier 1962–1983,* hrsg. von / ed. by André Kamber und / and Christine Kobel, Ausst.-Kat. / exh. cat. Kunstmuseum Solothurn, Solothurn.

1982 *John M Armleder / Martin Disler / Helmut M Federle,* Ausst.-Kat. / exh. cat. Centre d'art contemporain Genève, Genf / Geneva.

1981 *30 Künstler aus der Schweiz,* hrsg. von / ed. by Peter Weiermair, Ausst.-Kat. / exh. cat. Frankfurter Kunstverein et al., Innsbruck und / and Wien / Vienna.

1980 *John M Armleder. 891 und weitere Stücke,* hrsg. von / ed. by Dieter Koepplin, Ausst.-Kat. / exh. cat. Kunstmuseum Basel, Basel.
Fluxus International & Co, Ausst.-Kat. / exh. cat. Musée Rath, Genf / Geneva 1980.
Schweizer Museen sammeln moderne Schweizer Kunst, Ausst.-Kat. / exh. cat. Kunsthaus Zürich et al., Zürich.

1976 *Schweizer Pavillon der 37. Biennale von Venedig,* Ausst.-Kat., Venedig / Venice.

1974 *Ambiances 74,* hrsg. von / ed. by Adelina Cüberyan u.a. / et al., Ausst.-Kat. / exh. cat. Kunstmuseum Winterthur et al., Winterthur.

1973 *8e Biennale des jeunes de Paris,* Ausst.-Kat. / exh. cat. Musée d'art moderne de la ville de Paris, Paris.

1972 *Xylon. Prix international de gravure,* Ausst.-Kat. / exh. cat. Musée d'Art et d'Histoire, Genf / Geneva.

Werkliste / List of Works

Ohne Titel (Furniture Sculpture) / Untitled (Furniture Sculpture), 1985
1 Konzertflügel, zum Teil bemalt / 1 concert grand piano, partly painted
ca. 120 × 200 × 250 cm
Sammlung / Collection Paul Maenz, Berlin
Abb. S. / Ills. pp. 6, 24/25, 36/37

Ohne Titel (Furniture Sculpture) / Untitled (Furniture Sculpture), 1997
Kunstfell, Holz, Seil / Faux fur, wood, rope
160 × 120 × 80 cm
Courtesy the artist
Abb. S. / Ills. pp. 24/25, 44

No Pain, Just Gain. No Pain, Just Gain. No Pain, Just Gain. (Furniture Sculpture), 2002
Wollteppich (Flokati) / Wool carpet (Flokati)
240 × 340 cm
Courtesy the artist
Abb. S. / Ills. pp. 24/25, 28/29, 32/33

Ohne Titel (Furniture Sculpture) / Untitled (Furniture Sculpture), 2002
Acryl auf Leinwand, originaler Egg Chair von Arne Jacobsen / Acrylic on canvas, vintage Egg Chair by Arne Jacobsen
200 × 300 × 130 cm
Courtesy the artist and Mehdi Chouakri, Berlin
Abb. S. / Ills. pp. 26-29, 32/33, 40/41

Lubaantun (Chantico), 2002
Wandmalerei, Silberfarbe / Wall painting, silver paint
Maße variable / Dimensions variable
Galerie Andrea Caratsch, St. Moritz
Abb. S. / Ills. pp. 24/25, 30/31

Lubaantun, 2002
Wandmalerei, Goldfarbe / Wall painting, gold paint
Maße variable / Dimensions variable
Galerie Andrea Caratsch, St. Moritz
Abb. S. / Ills. pp. 26–29, 32/33, 40/41

Lubaantun, 2002
Wandmalerei, Elfenbeinfarbe / Wall painting, ivory paint
Maße variable / Dimensions variable
Galerie Andrea Caratsch, St. Moritz
Abb. S. / Ills. pp. 34/35, 40/41

AA (Furniture Sculpture), 2004–2008
Schrank (entworfen von Alvar Aalto für das Paimio Sanatorium, Finnland, 1928–1933), geformtes Sperrholz, weiße Wandfarbe, Leinwand, Spiegel / Closet (designed by Alvar Aalto for the Paimio Sanatorium, Finland, 1928–33), shaped plywood, white wall paint, canvas, mirror
204 × 280 × 35 cm
Courtesy the artist and Mehdi Chouakri, Berlin
Abb. S. / Ills. pp. 28/29, 32/33, 42

Ohne Titel / Untitled, 2010
21 Neonröhren mit Klammern (blau, dunkelrosa, rosa, grün, weiß) / 21 neon tubes with brackets (blue, dusky pink, pink, green, white)
Maße variable / Dimensions variable
Courtesy the artist
Abb. S. / Ills. pp. 24/25, 38/39

Let it ride (Furniture Sculpture), 2012
2 Rutschen (espas), Acryl auf Leinwand / 2 slides (espas), acrylic on canvas
344 × 273 × 316 cm
Courtesy the artist and Mehdi Chouakri, Berlin
Abb. S. / Ills. pp. 26–29, 32/33

G.R., 2016
Airbrush auf Aluminium / Airbrush on aluminum
200 × 130 cm
Courtesy the artist and Mehdi Chouakri, Berlin
Abb. S. / Ills. pp. 34/35, 40/41

G.S., 2016
Airbrush auf Aluminium / Airbrush on aluminum
200 × 130 cm
Courtesy the artist
Abb. S. / Ills. pp. 34/35, 40/41

S.A., 2016
Airbrush auf Aluminium / Airbrush on aluminum
200 × 130 cm
Courtesy the artist
Abb. S. / Ills. pp. 34/35, 40/41

J.M., 2016
Airbrush auf Aluminium / Airbrush on aluminum
200 × 130 cm
Courtesy the artist
Abb. S. / Ills. pp. 34/35, 40/41

Divino, 2019
Mischtechnik auf Leinwand / Mixed media on canvas, 350 × 700 cm
Courtesy of the artist and David Kordansky Gallery, Los Angeles
Abb. S. / Ills. pp. 24/25, 30/31

Installation CA.CA. 1, 2019
20 Spiegelglaskugeln / 20 Mirror glass balls
Maße variable / Dimensions variable
Courtesy the artist
Abb. S. / Ills. pp. 4, 10/11, 48/49

Installation CA.CA. 2, 2019
Gerüstbau, echte und falsche Pflanzen / Scaffolding, real and fake plants
Ca. 300 × 300 × 720 cm
Courtesy the artist
Abb. S. / Ills. pp. 24/25, 28/29

Vergleichsabbildungen / Text illustrations

John M Armleder mit / with *Furniture Sculpture*
Das Foto entstand im Rahmen des Kulturfestivals *steirischer herbst '82* in Graz / The photo was shot at the cultural festival *steirischer herbst '82* in Graz
Abb. / fig. 1

John M Armleder
Conversation, Etude pour John Cage sur dix bandes magnétiques, 1973
10 Schwarzweißfotos, Kassettenrekorder und Bänder/ 10 b/w photos, cassette player and tapes
Courtesy Mamco, Genf / Geneva, und der Künstler / and the artist
Abb. / fig. 2

John M Armleder
Furniture Sculpture 132, For the love of Daisy, 1986
Tempera und Acryl auf Leinwand, Washburn-E-Gitarre / Tempera and acrylic on canvas, Washburn electric guitar; Leinwände / canvases: 300 × 150 cm, 300 × 170 cm
Musées d'art et d'histoire, Genf / Geneva
Abb. / fig. 3

Francis Picabia
Volucelle [II], 1923
Emailfarbe auf Leinwand / Enamel paint on canvas, 198,8 × 250,2 cm
Privatsammlung / Private collection
Abb. / fig. 4

Larry Poons
Untitled (18-A), 1976
Acryl auf Leinwand / Acrylic on canvas, 288,3 × 205,7 cm
Museum of Fine Arts, Houston, Texas, USA
Abb. / fig. 5

Morris Louis
Beta Zeta, 1960/61
Acryl auf Leinwand / Acrylic on canvas, 255,3 × 439,4 cm
Nationalgalerie, Staatliche Museen zu Berlin
Abb. / fig. 6

John M Armleder, Collier Schorr – Brioni, Kampagne Herbst/Winter 2015 / Campaign fall/winter 2015
Abb. S. / Ill. p. 21

John M Armleder, Ausstellung / Exhibition *Peinture abstraite,* Genf / Geneva 1984
Abb. S. / Ills. pp. 23, 59

Impressum / Colophon

Dieser Katalog erscheint anlässlich der Ausstellung / This catalogue is published in conjunction with the exhibition

John M Armleder. CA.CA.

Schirn Kunsthalle Frankfurt
7. Juni bis 1. September 2019
June 7 to September 1, 2019

Herausgeberin / Editor
Ingrid Pfeiffer

Redaktion / Editing
Ingrid Pfeiffer, Rebecca Herlemann

Publikationen & Schirn Magazin / Publications & Schirn Magazine
Antonia Lagemann, Anuschka Berthelius

Lektorat / Copy editing
Karin Osbahr (Deutsch / German)
Lizzie Gilbert (Englisch / English)

Übersetzung / Translation
Gérard Goodrow (Deutsch–Englisch / German–English)

Gestaltung / Graphic Design
stapelberg&fritz, Büro für Gestaltung

Fotografien / Photographs
Norbert Miguletz

Lithografie / Reproductions
Cantz Medienmanagement, Esslingen

Papier / Paper
Magno Gloss, 170 g/m²

Herstellung / Production
Edition Cantz, Esslingen

Druck / Printing
Dr. Cantz'sche Druckerei Medien GmbH, Esslingen

Buchbinder / Binding
IDUPA Owen / Teck

Erschienen bei / Published by
Edition Cantz
Dieselstr. 50
73734 Esslingen

www.edition-cantz.de

ISBN 978-3-947563-47-0

Printed in Germany

Umschlagabbildung / Cover illustration
John M Armleder
Divino, 2019 (Detail)
Foto / photo: Julien Gremaud

Fotonachweis / Photo Credits
Es wurden alle Anstrengungen unternommen, um die Urheberrechtsinhaber zu ermitteln und die Abdruckgenehmigungen zu erhalten. / Every effort was made to identify and contact all right holders.

bpk / Nationalgalerie, SMB, Verein der Freunde der Nationalgalerie / Jörg P. Anders, S. / pp. 17, 55 rechts / right

Foto / photo: Collier Schorr, S. / p. 21

© Archives Ecart, Geneva, S. / pp. 15, 53

© Musées d'art et d'histoire, Ville de Genève, Foto / photo: Georg Rehsteiner, S. / pp. 16, 54 links / left

Museum of Fine Arts, Houston, Texas, USA / museum purchase funded by the National Endowment for the Arts and the Friends of Modern Art, by exchange / Bridgeman Images, S. / pp. 17, 55 links / left

Archiv / Neue Galerie Graz, Universalmuseum Joanneum, S. / pp. 12, 50

© Schirn Kunsthalle Frankfurt, 2019, Fotos / photos: Norbert Miguletz, S. / pp. 4, 6, 10/11, 24-42, 44, 48/49

Foto / photo: Jean-Francois Schlemmer, Genf / Geneva, S. / pp. 23, 59

Courtesy of Sotheby's, S. / pp. 16, 54 rechts / right

AUSSTELLUNG / EXHIBITION
SCHIRN KUNSTHALLE FRANKFURT

Direktor / Director
Philipp Demandt

Kuratorin / Curator
Ingrid Pfeiffer

Kuratorische Assistenz / Curatorial Assistant
Rebecca Herlemann

Ausstellungsleitung / Head of Exhibitions
Esther Schlicht,
Anna Noll (Assistenz / Assistant)

Organisation / Registrars
Karin Grüning, Elke Walter, Luise Leyer

Leitung Hängeteam / Supervision Installation Crew
Andreas Gundermann

Restaurierung / Conservators
Susanne Silbernagel

Technische Leitung / Technical Services
Christian Teltz, Oliver Taschke

Ausstellungsgrafik / Exhibition Design
Studioheyhey, John Russo

Presse / Press
Johanna Pulz, Julia Bastian,
Elisabeth Pallentin, Isabelle Hammer

Marketing
Luise Bachmann, Hannah Ruiz,
Heike Stumpf, Elena Schmidt

Sponsoring
Julia Lange, Miriam Werner

Pädagogik / Education
Chantal Eschenfelder, Simone Boscheinen,
Laura Heeg, Irmi Rauber, Olga Shmakova

Veranstaltungen & Besuchermanagement / Events & Visitor Management
Ute Seiffert, Lena Sobczinski

Verwaltung / Administration
Heike Berndt, Claudia Kroh,
Tanja Stahl

Assistenz Direktion / Assistant to the Director
Daniela Becker

Leitung Gebäudereinigung / Cleaning Supervision
Rosaria La Tona

Empfang / Reception
Bettina Beyermann, Vilizara Antalavicheva,
Josef Härig

PARTNER / PARTNERS

Corporate Partner der Schirn Kunsthalle Frankfurt / Corporate Partners of the Schirn Kunsthalle Frankfurt
Bloomberg L.P.
Commerz Real AG
HEUSSEN Rechtsanwaltsgesellschaft mbH
Le Méridien Frankfurt
Messe Frankfurt GmbH
Oliver Wyman GmbH
PPI AG
PwC
Wallrich Wolf Asset Management AG

Partner der Schirn Kunsthalle Frankfurt, des Städel Museums und der Liebieghaus Skulpturensammlung / Partners of the Schirn Kunsthalle Frankfurt, the Städel Museum, and the Liebieghaus Skulpturensammlung
Allianz Global Investors
Fraport AG
Samsung Electronics
Stadt Frankfurt am Main

Kulturpartner / Cultural Partner
hr2-kultur